BIBLE STUDY COMMENTARY

Mark

Bible Study Commentary

Mark

M. WILCOCK

130 City Road, London EC1V 2NJ

Fort Washington, Pennsylvania 19034

© 1982 Scripture Union
130 City Road, London EC1V 2NJ

First published 1982

ISBN 0 86201 116 7 (UK)
　　　0 87508 167 3 (USA)

Phototypeset in Great Britain by
Input Typesetting Ltd., London SW19 8DR.

**Printed in Great Britain by
Ebenezer Baylis & Son Limited
The Trinity Press, Worcester, and London.**

General Introduction

The worldwide church in the last quarter of the twentieth century faces a number of challenges. In some places the church is growing rapidly and the pressing need is for an adequately trained leadership. Some Christians face persecution and need support and encouragement while others struggle with the inroads of apathy and secularism. We must come to terms, too, with the challenges presented by Marxism, Humanism, a belief that 'science' can conquer all the ills of mankind, and a whole range of Eastern religions and modern sects. If we are to make anything of this confused and confusing world it demands a faith which is solidly biblical.

Individual Christians, too, in their personal lives face a whole range of different needs – emotional, physical, psychological, mental. As we think more and more about our relationships with one another in the body of Christ and as we explore our various ministries in that body, as we discover new dimensions in worship and as we work at what it means to embody Christ in a fallen world we need a solid base. And that base can only come through a relationship with Jesus Christ which is firmly founded on biblical truth.

The Bible, however, is not a magical book. It is not enough to say, 'I believe', and quote a few texts selected at random. We must be prepared to work with the text until our whole outlook is moulded by it. We must be ready to question our existing position and ask the true meaning of the word for us in our situation. All this demands careful study not only of the text but also of its background and of our culture. Above all it demands prayerful and expectant looking to the Spirit of God to bring the word home creatively to our own hearts and lives.

This new series of books has been commissioned in response to the repeated requests for something new to follow on from Bible Characters and Doctrines. It is now over ten years since the first series of Bible Study Books were produced and it is hoped the new books will reflect the changes of the last ten years and bring the Bible text to life for a new generation of readers. The series has three aims:

1. To encourage regular, systematic personal Bible reading. Each volume is divided into sections ideally suited to daily use, and will normally provide material for three months (the exceptions being Psalms and 1 Corinthians-Galatians, four months, and Mark and Ezra-Job, two months). Used in this way the books will cover the entire

Bible in five years. The comments aim to give background information and enlarge on the meaning of the text, with special reference to the contemporary relevance. Detailed questions of application are, however, often left to the reader. The questions for further study are designed to aid in this respect.

2. To provide a resource manual for group study. These books do not provide a detailed plan for week by week study. Nor do they present a group leader with a complete set of ready-made questions or activity ideas. They do, however, provide the basic biblical material and, in the questions for further discussion, they give starting points for group discussion.

3. To build into a complete Bible commentary. There is, of course, no shortage of commentaries. Here, however, we have a difference. Rather than look at the text verse by verse the writers examine larger blocks of text, preserving the natural flow of the original thought and observing natural breaks.

Writers have based their comments on the RSV and some have also used the New International Version in some detail. The books can, however, be used with any version.

Introduction

It is generally reckoned that the Gospel of Mark is the oldest of the four. We should be wrong, however, to assume on that account that it was also the simplest and the least sophisticated. Mark certainly produced the shortest Gospel, and in that sense his is a ready introduction to the good news of Jesus for those who are unfamiliar with it. But he is no naive story-teller. He has his own line and follows it. Matthew, Mark, Luke, and John are often said to portray Christ as respectively King, Servant, Man, and God; and the second of these portraits is particularly that of the *suffering* Servant prophesied by Isaiah. We see on the one hand Jesus suffering on behalf of his people (10:45); his death is at the heart of the good news which Mark is recounting (1:1). On the other hand Jesus suffers as an example to his people. Mark's readers were almost certainly Christians facing persecution in Nero's Rome, thirty years after the resurrection. They needed the encouragement of knowing that their tribulation was no strange thing, but the trial their Lord had already gone through and emerged from victoriously. This is why this Gospel still speaks especially clearly in times of difficulty and testing.

A number of helpful commentaries have appeared over the last twenty-odd years. Alan Cole's is approachable as well as thorough. William Barclay concentrates more on illustration and application; in the opposite direction, C.E.B. Cranfield and Eduard Schweizer go into greater theological detail. (R.P. Martin's *Mark, Evangelist and Theologian*, of similar weight, is not a commentary but a study of Mark.) An excellent recent work is that of W.L. Lane, to whom the following notes owe much. But in the end not even Lane's 650 pages are as valuable as the sixteen short chapters of the Gospel itself, as it sets before us so concisely and powerfully the way of the Servant.

Palestine in the time of Jesus

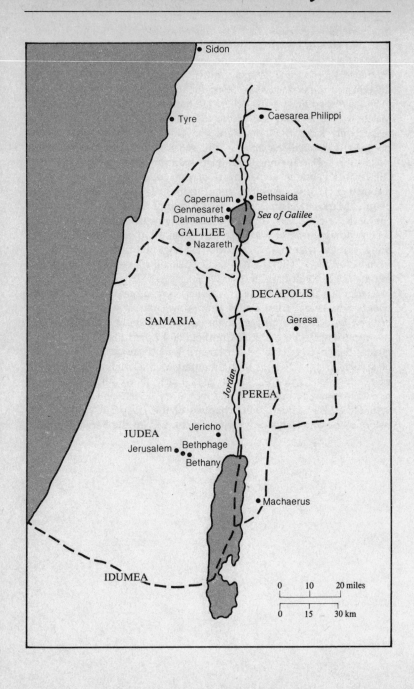

Analysis of Mark's Gospel

1:1–13   **In the Wilderness**

        1:1–13   The beginning of the Gospel

1:14–3:6   **In Galilee**

        1:14–2:12   The beginning of Jesus' deeds
        2:13–3:6   The beginning of Jesus' words

3:7–6:6   **Around the Sea of Galilee**

        3:7–35   A wider ministry
        4:1–34   Words about the kingdom of God
        4:35–6:6   Deeds against the power of evil

6:7–9:13   **Beyond Galilee**

        6:7–8:26   The question: who is Jesus?
        8:27–9:13   The answer: he is the Christ

9:14–10:52 **From Galilee to Jerusalem**

        9:14–10:52   The training of the disciples

11:1–16:8   **In Jerusalem**

        11:1–12:44   Challenge and conflict
        13:1–37   The Olivet discourse
        14:1–15:47   The suffering and death of Jesus
        16:1–8   The resurrection of Jesus

16:9–20   **An anonymous postscript**

1:1–8 John in the wilderness

What a resounding start to the Gospel (compare Gen. 1:1; John 1:1)! And a strange start, too. The good news concerns a person, Jesus, to be recognised eventually as Christ (8:29) and Son of God (15:39); but it begins with a place, the wilderness.

There first John appears. The biblical background to his coming is the Old Testament theme of an exodus through the wilderness out into a new life. As a future hope, this theme is found pre-eminently in Isaiah (hence v.2), though other scriptures are of course bound up with it (Isa. 40:3; Exod. 23:20; Mal. 3:1).

Whatever baptism may have meant elsewhere, John's was something so special that he actually became known as 'John the Baptiser'. It was a baptism of *repentance*, meaning that 'all the people' needed to confess their rebellion against God, and to go back, so to speak, to the Exodus-baptism of the Red Sea and the wilderness encounter with God. In that humiliation lay the hope of a new beginning.

This new start will become possible with the mysterious person who, though John's 'follower', will nevertheless be 'mightier' than he. For John is not only a fulfiller of the wilderness scriptures and a preacher of wilderness baptism; he is a prophet in the great wilderness tradition of Elijah, even dressed like that historic figure (2 Kings 1:8), and thus bringing the lessons of the past with startling clarity into the present. 'The meaning of Moses, Elijah, Isaiah, Malachi, comes alive in John the Baptist,' Mark tells his readers, as if to say that by the same token it is of course a living message to them too.

John looks back over the past, and forward to the future. He is, as it were, the signboard at the approach to a city: unlike the series of signposts which have pointed us towards our destination, he indicates that we have now reached it. He is not himself that destination, but simply proclaims it, as it looms up immediately beyond him. The immediacy, the vivid actualisation, is not only Mark's natural style, but his deliberate object. He wants us to encounter, beyond the servant, the Master (7); beyond water-baptism, Spirit-baptism (8). By the same Spirit who led his people through the original wilderness experience (Isa. 63:10–14), Jesus can lead men into a new life today.

THOUGHT: Before God's Spirit can lead us into new life we must face up to the demands of that new life and repent of our failure to meet them.

1:9–13 Jesus in the wilderness

As in prophecy (3), so now in fact, the herald is followed by the Lord: where John is, in the wilderness (4), there Jesus also comes.

These verses contain a series of contrasts. First is that between the two roles of Jesus: baptiser (8) and baptised (9). Rather as John stands between the old age and the new, appearing to each as part of the other, so Jesus stands between God and man, representing each to the other. As God, he will be Baptiser. For the moment, as Man, he is baptised, accepting that sin (not that he has any of his own) is under divine judgement, and that restoration is only by divine grace.

Contrasted also are those who come to John's baptism: the many from pious Judea, and the one from irreligious Galilee (5, 9). There is yet another contrast: the many confess but we do not hear God accept, God accepts the One even though we have not heard the Man confess. Jesus is the one Israelite truly submitted to God's will. So his Father is pleased (11) to appoint him the task of remaking the broken relationship between him and his people.

The wilderness, where their sonship was made (Hos. 11:1), is where it must be remade. Jesus is already there (4, 9), but this corner of it is by now rather crowded! So the Spirit drives him out into its solitudes. 'Immediately', which implies a close connection not necessarily in time only, but also in meaning ('it follows that'), is a favourite word with Mark; and 'it follows that' Jesus must establish himself, like Moses and Elijah with their forty days (Exod. 24:18; 1 Kings 19:4, 8) as a Wilderness Man. There, away from the world, but in the presence of God, the main lines of his coming ministry are laid down. Unlike Matthew and Luke, Mark is not concerned with the particulars of this period. For him, the conflict with Satan will in a sense continue throughout the Gospel, as if vs. 12, 13 were a newspaper headline and everything else were a long article telling the same story in detail. For sixteen chapters Jesus will experience on the one hand the beasts and on the other the angels. So in their turn will those for whom Mark writes, whether in his own age or since – all who (in Bunyan's words) are travelling 'through the desert of this world' towards their final salvation.

THOUGHT: 'Although he was a Son, he learned obedience through what he suffered' (Hebrews 5:8).

1:14–20 The Galilean ministry begins

Once John is 'delivered up' (14, RV), the last signboard is passed and we reach our destination. From this point on we are with Jesus himself, until he in his turn is delivered up (15:1, 15).

With Jesus' preaching of the gospel the new age bursts in upon men. His ministry is in a special sense a Galilean one. If the lower Jordan Valley, the background to 1:1–13, represents the wilderness, then 'Galilee of the Gentiles' (Matt. 4:15) represents the world. In the one, we see spiritual truth in all its clarity; in the other, human life in all its confusion. Nazareth of Galilee was Jesus' home (9). Bethlehem of Judea had been his birthplace, but Mark is not concerned with that; the fact he notes is, as John would put it, that Christ came 'into the world ... became flesh and dwelt among us' (John 1:9, 14). So now it is in Galilee that Jesus begins to preach (14, 15) and to call his disciples (16–20).

Here in the world of men he announces the good news. 'The time', the climax of all past times, the goal of Old Testament history and prophecy, has now fully come; 'the kingdom', the rule of God foreshadowed in the past story of Israel, is now with us – not yet, indeed, in such irresistible power that it sweeps all before it, but so close, nevertheless, that it confronts men with a crisis of decision. Hence the call to repent and believe.

There will be an interval between this arrival of the kingdom and its final consummation. So here in Galilee, in the world of men, he begins to choose those who, during that period, will follow him in the work of preaching the good news of the kingdom. These disciples will be fishers of men, not simply as a whimsical pun on their present trade, but because of the biblical background to this metaphor. Against that background, fishing for men is seen to be a matter of *judgement* (Jer. 16:16; Ezek. 29:4, 5). The net is not conversion, but confrontation with the gospel. This has a double effect (compare 2 Cor. 2:15, 16; 1 Pet. 2:6–8): while all the fish come under scrutiny, some are kept and others are rejected (Matt. 13:47–50).

THOUGHT: Like the fishermen, we may not understand all that is involved in Jesus' call. But their immediate and wholehearted response is a thing to be imitated.

1:21–28 The fishing begins

Back into the Galilean town of Capernaum, home of Simon and Andrew (29) and no doubt also of James and John, the 'fishers of men' make their way. The first thing that happens there puts flesh on several of the ideas which Mark introduced at the start of his Gospel.

Here is Jesus' conflict with the power of Satan (compare 1:13). In the Gospels, demon-possession is a reality distinct from illness (see also 1:32, 34; 6:13). One difference is the way the Lord is addressed in each case (contrast, for example, 3:11 with 10:47–52), possession being distinguished by what seems to be a separate personality speaking through the sufferer's mouth – a phenomenon noted also by modern investigators. The miracle so impresses the people that they see Jesus not simply as the exorciser of this particular demon, but as the kind of person who surely has authority over demons in general (27).

Here, too, is Jesus' proclamation of the gospel of the kingdom (compare 1:14, 15), both in word (21, 22) and in deed (27). Notice the reaction of the people in each case. Mark often mentions such reactions, and the various words he uses suggest not so much surprise as consternation, or even dismay. Jesus has authority not merely greater than one would expect in a village carpenter, but greater even than that of the official teachers of religion. Never before have they heard anything of the kind: he sounds disconcertingly like a prophet of old, with a message direct from God. He declares the rule of God to be something of far more than academic importance. It confronts them as a stark, immediate, and demanding reality.

In this way the 'Galilean' and 'fishing' themes also begin to be illustrated (see notes on 1:14, 16–20). As it should have been doing ever since, and should be doing even now through us, the net of Jesus' message goes forth; it spreads out into the world, 'throughout all the surrounding region' (28), reaching out to mankind in all its variety and all its need, and men are caught and held by it and drawn out into the light. The world hears the word: the fishing of Galilee has begun.

THOUGHT: 'You have heard that it was said ... but I say to you' (Matt. 5:21, 27, 31, 33, 38, 43). 'For I have not spoken on my own authority; the Father who sent me has himself given me commandment what to say and what to speak' (John 12:49).

1:29–39 Twenty-four hours at Capernaum

The healing of Peter's mother-in-law perhaps begins to teach him and his friends lessons to which the Lord will return in chapter 10. Peter, who has been called to leave his home, is taught that Christ is no man's debtor: where disciples learn to renounce, the Lord promises to restore (10:28–31). When Peter's mother-in-law is restored, her response is to serve: and the ideal of service is what James and John have to be taught (10:35–45). Both renunciation and service will in fact turn out to be keynotes of this Gospel.

Jesus has had no hesitation in dealing with both demon and disease on the Sabbath. The crowds, inhibited by the rules about Sabbath-breaking, wait till sunset, when the next day officially begins, and then come in droves to seek healing from him. We might say in charity that they cannot be expected to have grasped yet his teaching about Sabbath-keeping (see 2:23–3:6). But in truth there is a more basic lesson they seem not to have grasped. The 'whole city' wants his ministry of healing; but his ministry of preaching is quite another matter – we have already seen how that fills them with consternation. They want the benefits, but not the disturbance (compare John 6:26). You cannot, however, have the one without the other.

If, therefore, we ask whether the events of these twenty-four hours can be regarded as a successful start to the ministry of Jesus, it looks as though, whatever the disciples may have learnt, the people in general are seeing only what they want to see. Disappointment peeps out between the lines of the final paragraph (35–39). Jesus withdraws to a lonely place; the countryside round Capernaum is generally cultivated, but he contrives to find somewhere which in the small hours of the morning will do for a 'desert' (35, RV), where he can exchange once more the confusion of the town for the clarity of the wilderness, and see things as they really are. It is as though the disciples find him and say, 'Everyone here seeks your *cures*,' and he replies, 'Then I must go to the next towns with my *message* – *that* is what I have come for.' The Galilean ministry must be preaching as well as healing (39).

THOUGHT: You cannot have the benefits without the disturbance.

1:40–45 A leper's cure, and its aftermath

After dealing with demon-possession and fever, Jesus next faces leprosy. As with fever, the Bible speaks of a symptom rather than a disease. What is meant here is any one of a range of skin conditions, not necessarily leprosy in the modern sense. But whatever might cause it, its effects were grim. The 'leper' became an outcast. The law provided both for those suffering from 'leprosy' (Lev. 13:45, 46) and for those who were cured of it (Lev. 14:1–32), but in practice cures hardly ever happened. Such a complaint well illustrates the power of Satan, and the healing of it the power of Christ.

Against this background two unexpected words stand out in Mark's description of Jesus, his indignation (41, NEB – probably the correct reading, rather than 'pity') and his sternness (43). He does feel pity, no doubt, towards the leper. But really it is Satan, the author of this living death as of all the evil that it symbolises, who is here confronted, and towards him Jesus feels furious indignation. John tells of the same divine anger at the grave of Lazarus (John 11:33, RV mg.). Forthwith the evil is dealt with.

Then, however, Jesus has stern words for the healed leper. It is a harsh term that Mark uses, and we may wonder why. Now that the man is cured, he is *not* 'to talk freely about it' (45), but simply to go through the correct procedure by which a priest will certify the cure. This will be 'a testimony unto them' – to the people, or to the priests (44, RV). This probably means a testimony *against* them, i.e. incriminating evidence. When the Jewish authorities come to deny the claims of Christ, they will have to face the fact that they themselves affirmed the cures which backed up those claims, and thus they will stand condemned (compare John 15:24).

Whether or not the erstwhile leper obeyed Jesus by going to the priest, he disobeyed him by spreading the story everywhere. The result was that in the towns to which Jesus came as a preacher of the gospel (38), he found himself mobbed as being primarily a miracle-monger. Even another retreat to 'desert places' (45, RV; not 'country') had crowds pursuing him for the wrong reasons. No wonder he had spoken sternly to the leper. His anger is deserved not only by his enemy Satan, but by a well-meaning friend who repays blessing with disobedience and thus hinders the work of the kingdom.

CHALLENGE: Ask yourself how, even when acting from the very best of motives, you might have hindered the work of the kingdom.

Questions for further study and discussion on Mark 1

1. Discuss the meaning of baptism today in the light of John's 'baptism of repentance for the forgiveness of sins' and the baptism of Jesus.

2. What was the importance of Jesus' time in the wilderness? What equivalents, if any, are there in our own Christian experience?

3. What is it that makes fishing an appropriate metaphor for proclaiming the gospel? How do we see the double effect (see note on 1:14–20) in the face of our own presentation of the good news?

4. Verses 14, 15 represent the first announcement of the good news of salvation. How far should they be a model for our preaching? How would you present verse 15 to a non-Christian with little church background?

5. Authority is not a popular concept today. Discuss what you understand by Jesus' authority, illustrating from this chapter. What does this authority mean for our world? How can we present Jesus as authoritative in a world which often resents authority?

6. In what sense might Jesus' ministry be disturbing (see notes on 1:29–39)? How is that disturbance felt today? What balance should we have between 'disturbance' and 'benefit' in our preaching of the gospel?

7. 'A well-meaning friend who ... hinders the work of the kingdom' (see note on 1:40–45). How does that happen today? How might it happen in our own lives or in our church?

8. What was the relationship of miracles to preaching in the ministry of Jesus? What part, if any, should the miraculous play in our proclamation of the good news today?

2:1–12 Healing and forgiving

When Jesus returns to Capernaum, 'preaching the word' (2) continues to be his prime concern, though the crowds still doubtless want the miracles rather than the message. There *is* a healing – of paralysis, as previously of possession, fever, and leprosy – but this incident is the first in a series in which the Jews' repeated question 'Why?' (7, 16, 18, 24) is dealt with by his *teaching*. Here his message concerns the forgiveness of sins.

The miracle involves a man who is in very great need. So helpless that it takes four friends to carry the dead weight of him, so desperate that they are prepared to climb the outside stairs to the flat roof and remove the tiles to let him through (Luke 5:19; the vivid detail is, for once, not Mark's), perhaps incapable even of believing on his own account ('Jesus saw *their* faith'), his obvious need is to be set free from his paralysis. Many therefore must have thought the words of Jesus in verse 5 irrelevant as well as blasphemous.

The general meaning of his two declarations to the paralytic (5, 11) is clear. Anyone could *say* 'Your sins are forgiven'; so this unverifiable word is linked with one which is immediately verifiable – 'Rise and walk'. Demonstrably the latter works; the conclusion must be that the former works also.

The scribes were right, of course, in saying, 'Who can forgive sins but God alone?' (7). But we may do them an injustice if we say that they ought therefore to have recognised Jesus as God. Both healing and forgiveness could be brought, in God's name, by a prophet (1 Kings 17:17–22; 2 Sam. 12:13). They may well have thought Jesus was claiming that kind of authority, a direct word from God which was a cut above their own second-hand teaching. To them, this was quite scandalous enough. But however the scribes took it, Mark expects his readers to draw the deeper conclusion. Verse 10a, a notoriously difficult passage, may be meant to be read as if it were a footnote, or put in brackets, and translated 'Note that the Son of man ... '. If so, it is not Jesus proving to the scribes, but Mark pointing out to his Christian readers, that when the gospel of the kingdom confronts the needs of men, it deals with sin as well as sickness, and the sin is the primary problem.

THOUGHT: '...his beloved Son, in whom we have redemption, the forgiveness of sins' (Col. 1:13, 14).

2:13–22 Feasting and fasting

We can approach this passage in various ways. From one point of view Mark is continuing to unfold the gospel of the kingdom. We have already seen that it confronts men with truth, restores them to wholeness, and cleanses them from sin. Now we are shown that it works with the toughest of characters, since it can transform even 'tax collectors and sinners': men cynically willing to collaborate with Romans and rob fellow-Jews, or deliberately flouting accepted standards of decent behaviour. We are further shown that Levi's feast (see Luke 5:29), rather than the Pharisees', or even John's fasting, is the appropriate response, for transformations like this are matters for joy, not mourning.

The feasting of some and the fasting of others provoke the second and third 'Why?' conversations (16, 18; compare v. 7). To explain why he mixes with bad company and why his disciples do not fast, Jesus claims for himself two roles. What sort of people surround a *doctor*? The sick. And a *bridegroom*? The cheerful! Joy for sinners, not gloom for saints, is what the gospel brings.

Following another line, it is interesting to notice that Jesus' questioners assume he is still basically one of them. 'It is because you presumably agree with us about *this*, that we don't understand why you do *that*.' Not only Jesus' conclusions, however, but also his premises, differ from theirs. Hence the 'new cloth' and 'new wine' sayings (21, 22). They cannot have the new *plus* the old; if they try to do so, the garment, or wineskin, of traditional beliefs will not survive the attempt. The gospel is a total *replacement* for the old way of thinking.

The claims of Jesus suggest a fourth approach. As with his authority to forgive sins (5–12), they can be taken at more than one level. His hearers would have agreed that a doctor's visit implies sickness in the house, and that a wedding is a joyful occasion. The aptness of these homely comparisons was plain to see. But with hindsight, Mark's readers can see deeper implications. Jesus the 'doctor' is distinct from both sick and well, sinful and righteous; Jesus the 'bridegroom' links himself with the biblical teaching about the marriage between *God* and his people (Isa. 54:5; compare 2 Cor. 11:2). Just who does he reckon himself to be?

THOUGHT: 'Joy for sinners...'

2:23–3:6 The Sabbath

The series of debates between Jesus and the Pharisees which began at 2:1 ends with two Sabbath-day incidents.

In the first, the Jewish objection to the disciples' plucking of grain is not of course that the grain belonged to someone else – the law allowed that (Deut. 23:25) – but that they were 'reaping' on the Sabbath (Exod. 34:21). Jesus' answer is to quote an instance in Old Testament times (v. 26b may mean 'In the "high priest Abiathar" section of 1 Samuel'; the reference is to 1 Sam. 21:1–6, though Abiathar himself does not appear till the following chapter) when a leader and his men could infringe the regulations – not specifically Sabbath rules, but rules of a similar kind – without being accused of impiety.

That is the last of the 'Why?' questions; in the one remaining incident (3:1–6) the Pharisees' objection is unspoken. Had they replied to verse 4, they would have said: 'Yes, it is lawful to do good on the Sabbath, provided it is indeed a matter of saving life; but in this case it isn't.' Jesus, angry and grieved that they should be so 'insensitive both to the purposes of God and to the sufferings of men' (W.L. Lane), side-steps their half-formed accusation by himself saying nothing about healing, but only issuing the unexceptionable command of verse 5.

The first incident illustrates his general teaching about the Sabbath: the object of Sabbath rules is human welfare, and that must be the prime consideration (2:27). (2:28 may be another footnote for Mark's readers, like 2:10a: a further aspect of Jesus' lordship is being pointed out to them, who recognise him as Son of Man, rather than to his contemporaries, who did not.) The second incident naturally includes the same truth; but the main point of it is that his enemies are silenced, and realising that there is no common ground between them and him, they begin to plot, 'on the Sabbath', ironically, 'to do harm' and 'to kill'. The parallel with the controversies of Mark 12, which also lead to the silencing of his enemies and their plotting to kill him, is presumably intentional on the part of Mark.

QUESTION: How far is Jesus Lord of our 'Sabbath'?

3:7–19a The next stage begins

The paragraph 3:7–12 begins a new section of the Gospel. Like 1:14, 15, it serves as a heading for the next two or three chapters, summing up the kind of events that Mark will be narrating in them. As those earlier verses indicated that the contents of 1:16–3:6 would be about the gospel and the kingdom, their meaning and their effects, so these verses promise more about the disciples and the crowds, and about what they heard and saw of Jesus, particularly his power over the forces of evil.

But in two ways this long section will differ from that one. First, Jesus' ministry is no longer directed to Galileans alone. The crowds which flock to him are from southern Israelite territory also (Judea), and even from 'regions beyond', to north (Tyre and Sidon), south (Idumea), and east (Transjordan). In due course Jesus himself will visit all these places, except, as far as we know, Idumea. But already it is clear that the spread of the good news was never intended to be restricted to the people of the Israelite heartland.

Secondly, this ministry is no longer to be carried on by Jesus alone. Already in chapter 1 he had called his first few disciples and promised to make them fishers of men; now he 'makes' the twelve – that is the word translated 'appointed' in verse 14. (Mark prefers the term 'twelve' rather than 'apostles'; the number is certainly meant to recall the tribes of Israel, as though the people of God is here being constituted afresh.) Their apostleship is described in the simplest words. They are called 'to be with him': that is their training, the first stage of which starts here and concludes at 6:6. Then they will be 'sent out to preach', in 6:7–13. Light is shed on their names and nicknames by related passages elsewhere (the lists of Matt. 10:2–4; Luke 6:14–16; Acts 1:13; also Matt. 16:17, 18; Mark 9:38; Luke 9:54; Bartholomew is no doubt the Nathanael of John 1:45–51, Matthew is the Levi of Mark 2:14, Cananaean is 'Zealot', either Simon's personal character or his political group).

Thus Mark's readers can see that the gospel is to be preached *to* others besides Jews, which should move all Gentile believers to gratitude; and *by* others besides Jesus, which should provoke them to consider their own evangelistic responsibility.

THANKSGIVING: 'Christ became a servant to the circumcised in order that the Gentiles might glorify God for his mercy' (Rom. 15:8, 9).

3:19b–35 Jesus explained away

Three accusations against Jesus are here introduced briefly – he is mad (19b–21), or possessed (22a), or a sorcerer (22b) – and then followed up, at greater length, in the reverse order.

Remembering that Jesus has just appointed the twelve, we note that he begins their training by facing them with their enemy. 'Beelzebub' or 'Demon Prince', the Jews may call him, but he is in fact the Satan of the wilderness (1:13). Jesus' own ministry had begun with a similar confrontation, making plain what the gospel of the kingdom is primarily up against (1:21–28). Jesus' answer to the accusation of sorcery, of using Satanic power, is that Satan's kingdom shows the strength of a united front rather than the signs of disunity which, on their theory, the scribes should expect (23–26).

The charge of demon-possession is a more serious reflection on those who level it at Jesus. It shows that they do not acknowledge the power which really does possess him. For he comes as the *opponent* of the 'strong man' Satan, that is, as the Holy One (1:24); and as a *stronger* than Satan, being, as John had said when giving him a similar title, the one who has the Spirit (1:7, 8). Persistently to deny ('they kept saying...' is the meaning of v. 30) that Jesus' words and deeds have the authority of God's Holy Spirit – that is the ultimate sin. The man who cannot be forgiven is simply the one who refuses to accept the gospel of forgiveness which Jesus, by the Spirit, brings (28–30).

The accusation of madness brings us back to Jesus' family and friends. Of course he upholds what the law says about family loyalty (7:10; Exod. 20:12; 21:17). But he knows, as the law also knows, that it may be overridden by a higher loyalty (10:28–30; Exod. 32:25–29; Deut. 33:8, 9). So when his human family will not recognise his divine authority (compare John 7:5), he does not hesitate to contrast them, 'standing outside', with those who are inside with him, as it were, and who accept the message of God (31–35). Significantly, it is a house belonging no doubt to two of his disciples which is now regarded as his home (19b; 2:1).

THOUGHT: If we do not face strong opposition from Satan might it be because our lives and our message do not provide a real threat to his ambitions?

4:1–9 A notable parable

Mark devotes the greater part of this chapter to recounting some of the parables which were Jesus' regular method of teaching (34). Most of his hearers were left to work out for themselves what he meant, but occasionally we readers of the Gospel are favoured with the kind of explanation which the disciples were given, and such is the case here. By stopping at verse 9, however, we put ourselves in the position of the original audience, and ask ourselves what we make of the story as it stands.

In length and complexity it comes halfway between brief proverbs like 'The Physician' (2:17) and long narratives like 'The Prodigal Son' (Luke 15:11–32). We have yet to see whether each item in it stands for something distinct, or whether the details are simply background for the making of one main point. Parables may come in any of these styles. The Old Testament contains such illustrations in similar variety; indeed, 'illustrations' as used by preachers today are perhaps a close modern equivalent.

Jesus' first two words, 'Hearken – behold' in the AV, are significant. He wants us to listen and look. 'Look, a sower': perhaps one was actually there on the hillside in sight of the crowds. The parables make homely comparisons with things and events that are known to everybody. At that level his hearers know exactly what Jesus is talking about, though with the lapse of time some things may seem strange to us (for example, the sowing of seed by hand, to be ploughed in afterwards, so you might well not know which ground would be productive).

But the audience is exhorted also to *listen*. For the parable has an inner meaning which is not obvious. It may have something to do with the variety of types of soil; or with the large proportion of seed that comes to nothing; or, conversely, with the enormous harvest that results from the seed that *does* grow – for often a parable has some startling twist to catch our attention, in this case the hundredfold increase (not of course 100%, but 10,000%!).

THOUGHT: In spite of the surprise, misunderstanding, and hostility which greeted Jesus, he would not explain himself more clearly. His continued use of parables underlines the necessity of our being attentive, receptive hearers.

4:10–20 Parable-teaching explained

These words of Jesus, spoken when he is away from the crowds of 4:1 and 'alone ... with the twelve' and others of his disciples, answer one question and raise another.

The disciples had apparently asked him both about the parable of the sower and about his use of parables in general. With regard to this particular parable, it would be gilding the lily to set about explaining his explanation. Verses 14–20 are sufficiently clear. We may, however, note where he lays the emphasis. Nothing at all is said about the identity of the sower; the seed is defined simply as the word, the message of the gospel; it is the soils which are dealt with at length, so presumably the main point of the story concerns the different ways in which the message is received.

Whereas Jesus' words about this parable are an answer to a question, what he says about his parables generally, in verses 11, 12, actually raises problems rather than answering them. Many readers are offended by his apparent claim to be teaching in this way deliberately so as to mystify people, and to prevent their understanding. Unless we are going to tamper with the text, however, we have to accept that this is very nearly what he *does* say, as he quotes Isaiah 6:9, 10.

In the context, in fact, this is what *has* to be said. As some soils are receptive to the seed and others are not, so there are some people who receive the word and others who do not. Another way to describe the situation is to say that some are inside the circle of faith and others are outside (like Jesus' unbelieving relatives; compare v. 11 with 3:31–35). The divine plan is that to the man who has faith, understanding also is given; from him who has no faith, understanding must be withheld, 'in order that men may be left sufficient room in which to make a personal decision' (C.E.B. Cranfield). It is never God's intention to make the truth so unmistakably clear that men have to accept it even if they don't want to. To those who by faith are inside, 'everything' – the whole gospel – will be explained (34). But to those whose unbelief keeps them outside, 'everything' is spoken in parables, which can be, and are, misunderstood (11).

QUESTION: What is the answer to the common statement: 'Give me some proof; then I'll believe'?

4:21–34 How the 'secret' will work out

Four short parables are grouped in these verses. Many such sayings of Jesus appear in the first three Gospels, in differing contexts. By recording these four in this setting, Mark seems to be indicating that the message of the kingdom, which many find such a mysterious secret, will not always be so.

A lamp, for example (21, 22), might for some reason be hidden temporarily, but it will in the end be brought out where all can see it and be illuminated by it, for that is its very purpose. (Jesus actually spoke of 'the' lamp, and of its 'coming' – perhaps a clue as to what, or whom, he means by it?).

As the lamp *will* ultimately shine out, so the parable of the measure (24, 25) tells us that a bountiful return *will* be given to those who are prepared to give heed to the gospel. In the terms of the previous section (10–20), the man who has a believing heart will be given also an understanding mind.

Thirdly, the sown field (26–29) has a power 'of itself' to produce results. Mark uses the interesting and unusual word *automatē* almost as though growth takes place automatically. Parallel with the day-to-day life of the farmer, the life of the seed is also progressing, much of it under the surface, till the harvest crop grows up plain for all to see.

The parable of the mustard ends the series (30–32). As a seed, it is tiny and easily overlooked. As a full grown shrub, it is so big – perhaps ten feet high – that birds will nest in it as they would in a tree.

Did the disciples think it strange that so important a thing as the message of the kingdom should seem, when it came into the world, so obscure or insignificant? Probably that was one reason why they 'asked him concerning the parables' (10). So Jesus reassures them that one day his message *will* shine out, *will* bring returns, *will* ripen to harvest, *will* spread its branches wide. The question men must ask themselves is this: Now, in the time of its apparent weakness and obscurity, how fully are they willing to accept it?

QUESTION: How confident are *you* of a great future for the kingdom of God?

Questions for further study and discussion on Mark 2:1–4:34

1. What was the place and purpose of healing in the ministry of Jesus? What does this say about the place it should have in the life of the church today?

2. What authority does the church today have to announce forgiveness of sins? On what conditions? How should we go about it?

3. Joy marked those who met Jesus (see 2:13–22). Trace other biblical references to joy. How far is this characteristic reflected in our churches today? How would you answer the charge, 'Christians are such joyless people'?

4. Are there any individuals or groups with whom we would not wish to be seen? Consider how far this has led to a failure to share with 'those who are sick'.

5. 'The gospel is a total replacement for the old way of thinking' (note on 2:13–22). How would that apply to a wealthy businessman, a black teenager from a depressed inner city, a surburban housewife and mother, who became Christians? How has it applied in the experience of various members of your group?

6. If the object of Sabbath rules is human welfare, how does that affect the Christian's attitude to Sunday sport, shopping, leisure pursuits? Can there, should there, be one rule for Christians and another for non-Christians?

7. What place should parables, stories and illustrations have in our preaching and teaching? How should they be selected and presented?

8. How far can we see the fulfilment of Jesus' message concerning the growth of the kingdom? It has been said that, 'This is a day of small things – we must learn to live with it' – how far would you agree?

4:35–41 The stilling of the storm

Mark's version of the stilling of the storm includes several touches which suggest an account by an eyewitness (presumably Peter; contrast Matt. 8:23–27; Luke 8:22–25). This vivid story teaches something both about the disciples and about Jesus.

The fact that Jesus explains everything to them (34) does not mean that the disciples understand everything, still less that they are mature enough to cope with everything. And it is in practical difficulties like the storm described here that their lack of understanding is shown up. They betray a curious mixture of reverence and rudeness towards Jesus. They know him well enough to believe that he can do something about the situation if he wants to, yet they do not hesitate to say accusingly, 'Are we to drown for all you care?' (Moffatt). In the parables earlier in this chapter he has been assuring them of the eventual triumph of his gospel of salvation, but what use is that if he cannot help in their immediate predicament?

In the event he is of course in control in both realms, the natural as well as the spiritual. They could see this in his person: here was a man able to sleep through a storm so violent that it terrified even a crew of experienced sailors. Even more plainly, they could hear it in his words, when he rebuked and silenced the storm (just as he did in cases of demon-possession, for example 1:25).

This was not simply a miracle. It recalled the power which in Old Testament times could control sea and wind (for example, Pss. 65:7; 107:28, 29). When the Red Sea, in particular, obeyed such a command (Exod. 14:21), it was the Lord God of Israel whose power was thereby made known. No wonder on this present occasion the disciples 'were filled with awe, and said ... "Who then is this?" ' (41).

Here, in fact, is the Lord whose power has been known and celebrated from the beginnings of his people's history, and the Saviour whose plan of salvation will culminate in the final deliverance from this world to the next. This is the Jesus who is with them in their present practical needs.

THOUGHT: The One who has met the needs of so many is unlikely to fail us in ours.

5:1–20 The demoniac of Gerasa

Here is another kind of storm, which like that of the last paragraph is quelled by the rebuke of Jesus.

Why was the man in this state? It was not his own fault; at least, he is not said to be responsible or to need forgiveness. It was partly the fault of the people of Gerasa, whose attitude must have aggravated his suffering. But the real cause of the trouble was the legion of demons that possessed him. It is with them and their activity that Jesus is chiefly concerned.

Why their name? A Roman legion was a force of over 6,000; the number of demons in the man was certainly exceptionally large. Another military unit to which the word might loosely refer consisted of 2,048 men, which would tally with the number of pigs into which the demons went. Or it may simply mean a horde of spirits all acting as one, like well-drilled soldiers. At all events, they had deprived the man of the priceless privilege of a single heart (Ps. 86:11; Jer. 32:39). The real 'he' ran to Jesus; the demoniac 'he' wanted nothing to do with the Lord.

The actions of Jesus are revealing. If the result of seeing the man seated, clothed, and healed was fear, it must have been because Jesus' deed seemed an impossible miracle – which in turn shows the extreme madness to which the demons had already driven their victim. What they would have gone on to do is indicated by the fate of the pigs. If we ask why Jesus did not banish the demons altogether, 'into the abyss' (Luke 8:31), the answer may be partly that it was not yet time for the final defeat of evil; but verse 13 may also be Jesus' way of showing that the object of the powers of evil is not only to spoil, but ultimately also to destroy, the works of God.

So his own object is the opposite: 'to destroy the works of the devil' (1 John 3:8), in the widest sense: It is worth considering what actually were the mighty deeds of Jesus which the healed man 'began to proclaim in the Decapolis'. The forgiveness of sins, though central to the Lord's plan of salvation, is not mentioned here!

QUESTION: If you were to tell 'how much Jesus had done' for you, where would you begin?

5:21–34 The woman with the haemorrhage

Sandwiches are a speciality of Mark's! Other examples are at 11:12–21 and 12:1–12. The most familiar one is here, with the story of the woman with the haemorrhage sandwiched between the two halves of the story of Jairus' daughter. At the outset, the child is at the point of death; but though it is an emergency, Jesus' response and Mark's account must be left till after the woman's need has been dealt with.

Apart from its impertinent tone, the disciples might have been excused for their question in verse 31. But the woman's touch was in fact distinguishable in at least three ways from that of the many others who were jostling Jesus in the crowd. First, it was deliberate, not casual; the woman hoped to obtain a cure by it, in a way that smacks of magic (results guaranteed by what *we* do – compare Matt. 6:7). But we cannot imagine the healing taking place thus automatically; so, secondly, the touch must have been backed by faith in Jesus. Thirdly, it did in fact have a result. 'Power' went 'forth from him', and in some way he felt it go.

But he would not let the woman go away under any misapprehension about what had happened. She was made to confront him and to hear his illuminating word (33, 34).

Mark gives his readers a fuller explanation still. For he sets the incident in a sequence of four (the storm, the demoniac, this woman, Jairus' daughter), so that we may consider the *kind* of things Jesus is doing. On the one hand, he deals with human isolation: his disciples alone in the boat, the man driven out from society, the woman 'unclean' and untouchable, the dead child and the bereaved parents. On the other hand, he confronts this as an evil which Satan has wrought, and shows again that he has come into the world to undo the works of the devil; but we notice again that to none of these people is attributed any blame for their situation. Nothing is said about sin or forgiveness. All of them might say with reason, 'Why has this happened to us?' Although as sinners we deserve nothing better, it is encouraging to know that Jesus can deal not only with sin and its consequences, but also with the evils we commonly call undeserved.

THOUGHT: Read Ephesians 2:11–22 as a comment on Jesus' dealing with isolated and alienated individuals.

5:35–43 Jairus' daughter

Jairus' daughter really was dead, whatever Jesus might mean by saying she was not. The friends by bringing the message, the mourners by their ridicule, and the parents by their eventual amazement, make it plain that she was. And all of them presumed that not even Jesus could cope with *this* situation.

Death is the last evil confronted by Jesus in this sequence of four (storm, demon-possession, sickness, death). Jairus has seen his victory in the third case, and the disciples have seen all the first three. Jesus can do great things; but can he do the greatest thing? In our own experience, something quite different may be the sticking-point; it may be a much lesser thing than death, but to our mind it is the matter in which even Jesus, for all that he has done for others, must admit defeat.

But we know from the apostle's words in 1 Corinthians 15:26 and from the Lord's actions here that nonetheless 'the last enemy' is 'to be destroyed'. And as a token of its ultimate destruction Jesus releases the child from its clutches. This *is* only a token – only temporary, only this individual – but a token sufficiently astounding to make the point that Jesus does have power over the last insuperable foe. As before, final victory is not yet. The demons of Gerasa were not at once sent into the abyss, but were allowed to wreak destruction on the pigs. Death is defeated in the case of Jairus' daughter, and in a few other instances in the Gospels (Luke 7:15; John 11:44), but still lies in wait for the majority of mankind. Jesus does however demonstrate that the victory *is* his, so that even its delays are under his control.

His frequent injunction 'that no one should know this' is particularly strange in this case. How could such a thing possibly be hushed up? Perhaps he had in mind that while all would see the result, namely the resuscitated child, the details of the actual deed were to be something private to parents and disciples – the believers, the 'insiders' (compare again 4:11). Those who have faith are given sight also (4:25).

THOUGHT: 'I am the resurrection and the life; he who believes in me, though he die, yet shall he live, and whoever lives and believes in me shall never die' (John 11:25, 26).

6:1–6 Nazareth rejects its greatest Son

From most points of view, Jesus' visit to 'his own country', which we may take to mean Nazareth (1:9, 24), could hardly be described as a success.

On his part there were no miracles to speak of. When we are told that he *could not* do such works there we are to understand, not that he is ever less than all-powerful, but that miracles performed against a background of utter unbelief (even Jesus marvelled at it) would be mere shows of magic; and that *could not* happen without making a nonsense of what he had come to do. As before (see notes on 4:11, 12), he will not put men in the position of having to acknowledge him even if they do not want to.

On the part of the people of Nazareth, there is no response. This is doubtless a later occasion than the visit described in Luke 4:16–30; the only close parallel is the proverb of verse 4, which Jesus could well have used more than once, and there does seem to be a development in Jesus' reputation between Luke 4:22, 23 and Mark 6:2, 3. Nazareth has now come to disapprove of him. Every phrase used about him in verse 3 could have offensive overtones. What is more, this is the Nazarenes' general attitude: in verse 2 'many' is '*the* many' ('the large congregation ... said ...', NEB).

But although the whole affair may seem something of a fiasco, it has its place in the Lord's overall plan. It completes the picture of his friends, his family, and now his fellow-citizens 'standing outside' (3:31; and compare 3:21) and not accepting his claims. And the rejection at home results in the spreading of the gospel farther afield. This incident will be followed by the sending out of the twelve. They in turn will be told to leave the unreceptive and to go on to preach to others (10, 11). Jesus' own final rejection, on Good Friday, will lead to the sending out of the church at Pentecost. Mark's readers are being taught to view their own troubles in the light of this broader plan.

QUESTION: Are we able to view our troubles in the light of God's broader purposes?

6:7–13 The sending of the twelve

The twelve are sent out as Jesus' representatives. Their mission is an extension of his.

This is clear first from the way Mark tells the story. Jesus' ministry begins in 1:14, and he preaches the gospel by word and deed until opposition to it crystallises in a plan to destroy him (3:6). From the start (1:16–20) he had called disciples to be with him; and next he chose twelve of them (3:14), and through a second sequence of words and deeds he set about training the twelve, until ever-increasing opposition culminated in his rejection at Nazareth (6:1–6). Now a third preaching of the gospel begins, but this time the twelve are doing it.

It is clear not only from the overall pattern of the story, but also from the details of this section, that the twelve are Jesus' ambassadors. They have the *same authority*: their being sent in pairs implies that their witness is true, as his is (Deut. 19:15; John 8:13–18). They have the *same dependence* on the Father: despite slight differences (Matt. 10:9, 10) and Luke (9:3) may be making the same point as Mark. For them the twelve are to rely on nothing at all except God, while Mark says that, *with* staff and sandals, the pattern of the exodus (Exod. 12:11) is to be repeated, with its utter trust in God (we recall the 'desert' theme of 1:12 and elsewhere). They have the *same programme*: to preach repentance, and to restore the suffering, showing that God's plan of salvation deals with both the sin for which we are responsible and the evil for which we are not. They cause the *same effect*: men are polarised and judged according to their acceptance or rejection of the message. As Jews would shake off from their shoes the dust of a pagan land when they left it, so the twelve declare that those who refuse the gospel, whether Jews or not, are 'pagans' and outsiders.

Their methods are not meant to be copied literally. This was a 'one-off' mission, as we can tell from Luke 22:35, 36. But in essence the mission of the church is the same now as then. For us the heart of the matter is that which their methods implied: truth, trust, the gospel, and the clarifying of ultimate issues.

THOUGHT: How do we show that our dependence is on God and not on material possessions?

Questions for further study and discussion on Mark 4:35–6:13

1. Do we sometimes feel that Jesus does not care? What should we do in such situations? What help does Mark give?

2. What makes various members of the group afraid? Do Christians differ from non-Christians in the fears they have? How might these chapters of Mark help with facing fear?

3. In recent years there has been an increased interest in the occult, the supernatural and the demonic. Why might this be? How should Christians respond? What guidance do we receive from the Gospels?

4. Who are the 'isolated' people in your community? What more could your church or group do to reach them?

5. In what ways are the 'works of the devil' seen today? How are we as the people of God continuing the work of Christ and putting right these evils?

6. How would you use the story of Jairus' daughter to help someone who had recently been bereaved? What is distinctive about the Christian's attitude to death?

7. Christian missionaries have sometimes been criticised for a life-style far above that of those to whom they have ministered. On the other hand they have often been expected to make much greater sacrifices than Christians who remain in 'normal' employment. How do our attitudes to mission compare with those of Jesus in sending out the twelve? Should only some make special sacrifices?

8. Church growth thought argues that we should concentrate our evangelistic efforts on the most receptive groups. At what point, if at all, should we stop trying to reach certain individuals or groups? What do Christ's instructions to the twelve say to us about this?

6:14–29 The passion of John

Since the death of his father, the Herod of Matthew 2:1, Herod Antipas had ruled Galilee and Perea. Unofficially, and in his own eyes, a 'king', he was strictly speaking only a tetrarch (ruler of one-fourth of the country). His wife Herodias had been married to his brother Herod Philip, the point of John's rebuke being that Philip was still alive (contrast Lev. 18:16 with Deut. 25:5). The girl, Salome, was their daughter, probably a teenager at the time of this incident and afterwards to be married to yet another of the Herods. The Jewish historian Josephus also tells the story, adding such details as the girl's name, the place (the palace-fortress of Machaerus, near the Dead Sea), and the political factors as well as the personal ones which made Herod imprison John.

Mark may have at least two reasons for telling this story at this point and at this length. For one thing, it fills in the background of Herod's reaction to the events of verse 13. They have raised the question 'Who is Jesus?' Most say, 'A prophet'; Herod, with his guilty conscience, thinks he knows *which* prophet (this story tells us why); the same question underlies the next two or three chapters, and emerges again to be answered finally at 8:27–29.

In addition, we may compare this passage with chapter 15. It is not mere fancy that sees here, parallel to the passion of Jesus, a 'passion' of John – quite literally, when we note how 'passive' he is, with the narrative concentrating on what is done to him, and what he suffers at the hands of others. Herod, unwilling but cornered; malicious Herodias; Salome, prompted to make the actual demand; the soldier who does the deed – these all have their counterparts in the later chapter, and lay down the pattern ('They did to him whatever they pleased', 9:13) of what is to happen to Jesus. Thus Mark is preparing for the revelation both of Jesus' identity and of his destiny. The latter, the suffering of the one who is altogether submitted to the Father's will, is to be one of Mark's main themes in the second part of his Gospel. Be warned! He will be making it clear that those who follow Jesus, as Jesus followed John, will have to go the same way.

THOUGHT: '...heirs of God and fellow heirs with Christ, provided we suffer with him in order that we may also be glorified with him' (Rom. 8:17).

6:30–44 The feeding of the five thousand

The immediate lesson of this, the only miracle narrated in all the Gospels, is that the Lord can provide for his people when they are in real need and when their own resources are hopelessly inadequate.

But there is more to be learnt than that. For instance, it is the busy ministry of the twelve (7–13, 30, 31) which leads first to their being given rest, and then to the crowds being given food, in 'a lonely place'. The blessing of the Lord's people in general is a sequel to the faithful service of his servants.

Secondly, the place: the people found themselves out in the pastures ('green grass', v. 39). It was not what we would call a desert (AV), but this 'lonely place' is all the same a 'wilderness', as in 1:13, 35. Men are led out of their old life to a place where they are alone with the Lord, become his people, and are blessed and fed by him – one of Scripture's constant themes. The five thousand illustrate what it means to be truly Israel, the people of God.

'Sheep without a shepherd' comes from Numbers 27:17 and Ezekiel 34:5. In the first of those chapters a leader, Joshua, and in the second of them a provider, David, is promised to the wandering sheep. The quotation is so apt, because in each passage God is caring for them *in the wilderness*. And Jesus is saying that this care is now to be found by coming out into the wilderness to *him*.

It might almost be said, in fact, that Jesus is for once consciously 'setting up' a miracle. Yet even this large-scale demonstration is so designed as not to compel the unwilling to believe. The fare is not exotic, just ordinary bread and fish – you could assume if you so wished that it had come from some quite ordinary source. The sign which the people saw and which prompted them to 'take him by force to make him king' (John 6:15) could have been merely his lavish provision for them; the miracle of *how* it had been done, which showed him to be not simply prophet (John 6:14) but Lord, was known only to the disciples. We have to believe in him before he will begin to prove himself to us.

THOUGHT: God's love and blessing are to be experienced in the wilderness.

6:45–56 Jesus walks on the water

There are two intriguing phrases found only in Mark's account of this miracle.

First, the disciples' amazement at it was because 'they did not understand about *the loaves*' (52). What has the feeding of the five thousand to do with Jesus' walking on the water? For Mark implies that if they had understood the one, they would not have been surprised at the other.

Neither was a mere miracle. Both were 'signs' – they signified something; and in a sense, both signified the same thing. In asking what they meant, we recall the other sea-miracle, when Jesus stilled the storm (4:35–41). That was one of a series in which the *word* of Jesus is shown to have power over all kinds of evil. But here it is not so much his word, as his *identity*; less the power that he has, than the person that he is. 'Who is he?' is the underlying question from 6:14 to 8:29. The loaves should have taught his disciples that the Lord who in the days of the exodus drew his people into the wilderness, and there sustained them miraculously, is present again, still caring for his people. So they might have expected his care to be demonstrated equally when they were in trouble on the sea.

This leads to the other strange phrase: 'he meant to *pass by* them' (48). Having just been told that he saw their distress and *came to* them, what are we to make of this? Some would translate differently – 'to pass their way'. But a more attractive suggestion recalls the same phrase where it occurs at two crucial points in the Old Testament. Both Moses and Elijah, those two key figures, experience the Lord's 'passing by', not at all in the sense that he is going to ignore them and leave them, but as a mighty demonstration that he is *there* in his greatness and glory. His servants need not fear nor be discouraged, since he is in control (Exod. 33:19–23; 1 Kings 19:11). Faith is the key (and vs. 55, 56 provide further examples of it).

THOUGHT: Those who trust him, whether Old Testament saints or storm-tossed apostles or Mark's original readers or ourselves, will find him such a Lord, however distressed in rowing they may be.

7:1–13 Two kinds of religion distinguished

Here is a new development: no longer simply *that* the Pharisees oppose Jesus, but *why* they oppose him. It is because two quite different systems are in collision, his new one and their old one (not the original faith of Moses and Isaiah, which Jesus endorses, but the Judaism that had grown out of it).

First, the new is *bigger* than the old. Notice the 'footnotes' which Mark appends to the words 'defiled' and *'corban'* (2b–4, 11; compare notes on 2:10, 28); these are technical terms, understood by the initiated but needing explanation for the wider world for which Mark is writing. Judaism is for an exclusive community, Christianity for everyone.

Next, the new is *more consistent*. The Pharisees' religion is supposed to derive from the original Law and Prophets; so Jesus appeals to these origins – to Moses (10; Exod. 20:12; 21:17) and Isaiah (6, 7; Isa. 29:13) – and shows how far the Jews have departed from them. The 'tradition of the elders' is the 'tradition *of men*', and still worse, *'your* tradition' (5, 8, 9), eventually going so far that it actually contradicts God's law. For example, a man who designates his property *corban*, that is, not available for normal use, does so on oath; and the rule about keeping oaths (Num. 30:1, 2) is taken by the Pharisees to nullify even the rule about caring for parents (Exod. 20:12). But we must not 'so expound one place of Scripture, that it be repugnant to another' (Article 20 of the Church of England). When men can thus make God seem to contradict himself, they show just how far from him they are (6). Those who truly love him will see that his word is all of a piece. In this case it should have been clear that any oath which deprived parents would not have met with God's approval in the first place.

Most important, the new is *deeper* than the old. The hand-washing rules which began the dispute were only one example of the whole Pharisaic 'walk' (5, AV), which reached out through so many areas and down through the generations (13). The trouble with the whole thing was that it dealt with the superficial cleansing of superficial defilement. To the deep need, and the deep answer, Jesus will address himself in the next section.

TO THINK OVER: How do these verses illustrate 2:21, 22?

7:14–23 The heart of the matter

What had sparked off the disagreement between Jesus and the Pharisees in this chapter was the disapproval they had expressed of his disciples' eating with unwashed hands (2). This passage completes his response to them. After his retort in verses 6–13, his actual answer to their question is spoken here in verses 14–23. And he speaks not to them but to the crowds. What he wants to say should be heard by as wide an audience as possible. We can sense its importance from his solemn command to 'listen', and from the cryptic nature of his 'parable', which is designed to make them think (14, 17; in 3:23 also the word 'parable' was used in this sense): 'What defiles a man is not what goes into him, but what goes out of him.'

Though many have heard the 'parable', only the disciples, inside the house with him (remember 3:31–35!), begin to learn its double lesson. One vital truth is in the matter of how we are to be reckoned clean or unclean in God's sight. In this, Jesus shifts the emphasis from right deeds to right desires. Of course 'doing the right thing' is important. But it is no use making sure that we have clean hands – that our activities are properly moral or religious – if we do not first have a clean heart.

The second truth was harder. Mark here puts it in a footnote to his readers: 'Thus he declared all foods clean' (19b). But even Peter did not grasp this till long after (Acts 10:9–15; 11:4–9; 15:7–9; Gal. 2:11–13), and Paul was still having to explain it in his letters (Rom. 14:14, 20; Col. 2:16, 21–23). In Old Testament days, the outward observances of religion had been binding on God's people. Now all such regulations were abolished. God's law was henceforth to be an inward thing (Jer. 31:33; Heb. 10:16). Only when it was understood that all Old Testament religious observance had been meant simply as a picture of spiritual realities, to be fulfilled in Christ, could the rightness or wrongness of an action begin to be determined not by regulations but by principles. We are free to do whatever is in our heart, provided our heart is right.

THOUGHT: 'Who shall ascend the hill of the Lord?...
He who has clean hands and a pure heart...' (Ps. 24:3, 4).

7:24–30 Blessing outside the Jewish law

Jesus' reaction to the Syrophoenician woman may seem harsh, even rude. But it becomes understandable when we remember how many people had been seeking him merely for his miracles. He needed to know whether this woman understood and trusted him for himself.

The remarkable thing was that she was a Gentile, one of the 'lesser breeds without the law'. She thus provided Jesus with a concrete example of what he had just been teaching (14–23). If we are 'defiled', and therefore rejected by God, is it because we fail to keep the rules or because our hearts are not right? Well, here was a woman who was outside the rules altogether! Yet in her non-Jewish heart were a faith and an understanding lacked by most law-abiding Jews.

In this way Mark opens the door on an exciting new view of the gospel. If God is looking for something other than a keeping of the law, and finds it in this woman who is right outside the law, then the gospel is available for the most unlikely people. The region Jesus was visiting was literally 'beyond the pale' (the 'borders' of Tyre and Sidon, v. 24, AV). But wherever he is, and wherever he finds real confidence like that shown by the woman who accepts his words and follows up their implications, there will be found a blessing which is denied to those who merely try to live by the rules.

She may possibly have taken 'children and dogs' to mean 'Jews and Gentiles'. On the other hand, she may have taken only the less sophisticated point that she, an intruder, could not claim quite the same relationship to Jesus as those who were already 'in the house' with him (compare 3:31, 32). But in either case she grasped that both children and pets are equally *dependants* in the household, and for those who depend wholly on him the Lord will surely provide.

CHALLENGE: Are we prepared to see the gospel reach 'the most unlikely people'? Do we share it with such people?

Questions for further study and discussion on Mark 6:14–7:30

1. Why should Herod see Jesus as a reincarnation of John? What does this tell us about guilt? Is it ever possible to silence the voice of God's messengers? What other examples can you find in the Bible and in church history?

2. Think about the wilderness and the 'lonely place' as themes in Scripture. What part do they play in the life of God's people then and now?

3. Compare the attitude of the disciples when confronted with the hungry crowd with that of Jesus. What do we learn from this about facing situations of great need? What such situations face us?

4. It has been said that you cannot preach the gospel to men with empty stomachs. What does the feeding of the 5,000 say about our priorities in evangelism and social care?

5. A group of teenagers was converted in an inner city area; because they did not instantly give up smoking, drinking and unconventional dress they found that no church would accept them. Does Mark 7:1–13 say anything about this situation? What would your church have done?

6. Have you ever been puzzled by verses of Scripture which seemed to disagree? Discuss instances within the group, helping one another to understand what God is really saying.

7. What is your first reaction to the statement, 'we are free to do whatever is in our heart, provided our heart is right' (notes on Mark 7:14–23)? Is this more or less demanding than obeying a set of rules? Discuss some of the practical problems involved.

8. For what reasons may people come to Jesus today? How, if at all, should churches try to sort out those with wrong motives? Discuss this in the light of the story of the Syrophoenician woman and your church's procedure for admitting new members.

7:31–37 See the promises come true

Jesus, taking the handicapped man aside, 'put his fingers in his ears … spat, and touched his tongue' (33). What was the meaning of the action? Not that Jesus' touch was magic, for it was his word of power which actually healed; nor that onlookers needed it as a visual aid, for it was done in private. Perhaps it was simply a way of telling the deaf man what Jesus intended to do (particularly as saliva was thought to have healing properties; see also 8:23).

What, more importantly, was the meaning of the miracle? Why does Mark record it – the only evangelist to do so?

True, it added another to the impressive number of Jesus' cures. But it was more than just another miracle. We might go on to say that like all the signs Jesus did it had a spiritual significance which corresponded to the physical event that had taken place. He himself tells us, for instance, that the healing of a blind man illustrates the fact that true 'sight' is his gift alone (John 9:1–7, 39). So here, we learn that he can give the spiritual equivalents of hearing and clear speech.

But the miracle means more even than that. We have to account for the reaction of the crowds once the miracle was known, and ask why they were 'astonished beyond measure'. The clue lies in the rhythmic words that came to their lips. For these come from the prophecy of Isaiah 35:5, 6. That passage in its Greek version is in fact the only other place in the Bible where Mark's very unusual word for a speech impediment is found, which suggests a deliberate connection between the miracle and the prophecy. And the latter was generally thought to foretell what would happen when Messiah came. In other words, people took the healing to be a claim that with Jesus the times of the Messiah had arrived. So a chapter and a half of the deeds of Jesus (6:31–7:37) are climaxed by public recognition that with him the promises are coming true. Strange that our praise and prayer are so often shaped by what we think he should do, rather than what Scripture has said he will do.

FOR PRAISE AND WORSHIP: Use Isaiah 35 as a base for praising God for all that he has done for you through Jesus the Messiah.

8:1–10 Repeating a lesson

The likenesses between the feeding of the 4,000 and that of the 5,000 (6:35–44) are obvious. So too are the differences – the numbers of people, loaves, and fish, and the amount of food left over (seven large baskets instead of twelve small ones). It is perverse to see these, as some do, as two versions of the same incident.

We can for one thing see a development from the first to the second. It is too neat to see in the first incident God's grace towards Jews and in the other his grace towards Gentiles, with much symbolism in the numbers, which is what some suggest. This latter feeding of a crowd from the mixed population of the Decapolis does, however, confirm the trend of chapters 7 and 8 towards an increasing sense of responsibility to the Gentiles.

In any case, Mark himself understood there to have been two feedings (see 8:19, 20). Indeed, compare 6:31–7:37 with 8:1–30 and you will see that he reckoned an entire sequence of events to have been repeated: crowds fed, Pharisees rebuffed, bread discussed, infirmity healed. That is, he saw this as part and parcel of Jesus' own teaching method. And since the Lord demonstrably *does* teach in this way, then the repetition of such a miracle is altogether likely, and is not a mistake or an invention of Mark's.

For not only in the Gospels do we find that the divine teaching covers the same ground again and again, but that throughout his revelation God works in this way. His written word is full of repetitions of the basic lessons concerning holiness and sin, judgement and grace. So too in the book of nature, in creation as well as redemption. All over the world every animal, every plant, is a variation on a constant theme, and throughout time every dawn is unlike, yet like, the one before. And just so we are not hungry once only, nor does God feed us once only, and there is nothing more likely than that he should have shown this aspect of his goodness in the two miracles before us. So we may expect him to provide for us today as he did yesterday.

PRAYER: 'Give us each day, our daily bread' (Matthew 6:11).

8:11–26 The indispensable extra touch

Like the earlier feeding of a crowd, the one in 8:1–10 leads on to an exposure of the Pharisees' unbelief and the disciples' lack of understanding (7:6, 7, 17–19).

The trouble with the Pharisees was that they would only believe if given a 'sign' – not a miracle such as they had already seen, but something more which would prove to their own satisfaction that the miracles were divine. This unbelief is like yeast in dough; it affects the whole of one's life. The trouble with the disciples was that they were preoccupied with their ordinary needs, and so teaching like this often passed them by. They heard what they wanted to hear, and presumably took Jesus' mention of yeast (15) to refer to the bread they had forgotten.

For those with eyes to see, there was a plain message in the two bread-miracles, brought out especially clearly by the amounts left over. On both occasions they should have grasped what it was they were seeing and hearing (18): namely, the abundant grace of God given to the world in his Son the Messiah (see comment on 6:45–56).

Amazing, one might think, that they should remember the facts, but miss the meaning? Not really; it simply highlights the total inability of even the most privileged people to grasp spiritual truth until God works a miracle in them. In the earlier sequence, the Syrophoenician woman was thus enabled to hear and speak truth; her experience was vividly embodied in Jesus' healing of the deaf-mute; the result was recognition of Jesus as Messiah (7:24–37). In this chapter, the healing of the blind man points us back to the other half of the messianic prophecy of Isa. 35:5, 6, and the result will be similar, the great confession of Messiah which stands at the heart of Mark's Gospel (see tomorrow's passage, 8:27–30).

But to acknowledge Jesus as Messiah the disciples need not only to see the facts, but to have their eyes opened to the meaning. To illustrate this, the healing of the blind man is, alone among the miracles, a two-stage process. It is only by the touch of Jesus that we come to see anything at all; but we need that indispensable extra touch to see things as they really are.

THINK: What are you missing through your preoccupation with ordinary needs?

8:27–9:1 The pivot of Mark's Gospel

The whole story so far has been moving towards the crucial event at Caesarea Philippi. Every possible hint has been given as to who Jesus is, and not one has been properly grasped, not even by those closest to him (21). But now Peter's eyes are miraculously opened, as Mark says in one fashion and Matthew in another (25; Matt. 16:17), and the great title, hidden all the way from 1:1 to 8:29, is at last uttered. The second half of the Gospel will be concerned with unfolding the meaning of Jesus' messiahship.

At once its two chief implications are stated 'plainly' (32). The Hebrew word Messiah and the Greek word Christ both mean 'anointed' – appointed, designated. Whether Jesus is anointed as prophet, priest, king, or all three, is not the first consideration. Whatever may be his ultimate glory, first he is to suffer. This is what God has decreed ('must', 31), so to suggest otherwise is the kind of thing Satan would say (33). Perhaps when Jesus tells Peter to get behind him, he means him to return to the humble, teachable position of a disciple, which is what the same Greek phrase means in the very next verse ('come *after* me'; similarly in 1:17, 20).

And what Peter must learn is a second lesson, besides the necessity of Messiah's suffering: namely, that for the followers of Jesus also the cross must come before the crown. 'The humiliation of the Messiah ... is the mysterious prototype of that of the Christian' (W.L. Lane). Nor is this for church leaders only, but for all who would follow him (34). A few of his hearers will be given a glimpse of the glory of the kingdom *before* they are called to follow the way of the cross. Jesus perhaps refers to the experience Peter, James, and John will have in a week's time on the Mount of Transfiguration. Nevertheless the call is to give up one's life for the sake of Messiah, and only afterwards to receive it back again.

THOUGHT: Even mature Christians may catch themselves complaining, 'Why should it happen to me?'. To remind ourselves of Jesus' shocking picture of 'the march to the scaffold' (34) will help us to accept our own troubles as an inevitable, and indeed primary, fact of Christian discipleship.

9:2–13 Gloom and glory

The previous passage helps us to see the purpose of the transfiguration. All the disciples' assumptions had been upset by what Jesus said about the path of suffering which both the Messiah and his followers would have to tread. They (and Mark's readers, for whom suffering was a more immediate problem) needed reassurance that things *would* work out in the end, that there *would* be a crown after the cross. The transfiguration is a preview of Jesus' return in glory, designed expressly for their benefit (2, 4, 7).

Mount Tabor, the traditional site of this event, is less likely than Mount Hermon, which is higher, remoter, and more in accord with Jesus' withdrawal to the far northerly region of Caesarea Philippi. It is a counterpart of Sinai/Horeb, that other mountain of revelation in the far south where both Moses and Elijah met God (Exod. 24; 1 Kings 19). We are back in the atmosphere of Mark's earliest chapters, with the theme of the wilderness, where, far from the distractions of the world, things can be seen as they really are, and the voice of God can be clearly heard (compare especially 1:1–13, and Jesus' baptism).

Yet Jesus has said that such mountain-top experiences will be the exception, and that discipleship is normally a hard way. The disciples still find this incomprehensible. They cannot square his gloomy talk of suffering, and having to rise from '*the dead*', with the glorious Messiah they have just seen and the prophecy about Elijah putting things right before Messiah comes (Mal. 4:5, 6).

To their astonishment, they learn that even their idea of Elijah the great restorer has to be turned upside down. John the Baptist was the one who filled the role, as had been hinted at the time (1:2–8). The work of restoration was in fact his preaching of repentance; and so far from a triumphant progress, even the new Elijah's way had been a way of suffering, with Herod and Herodias stepping into the shoes of Ahab and Jezebel.

THOUGHT: We, like Mark's readers, must not be surprised if the Christian way is not easy. Neither the Lord, nor his forerunner, nor his followers, found it so. We no longer see the glory, and will not see it until the end. But we do still hear the reassuring word, and are in good company.

9:14–29 Prayer the key to power

Another link between Jesus' transfiguration and his baptism, in addition to those already noted, is that each great experience of God was followed immediately by conflict with Satan. The conflict which follows now is related to the recent mountain-top events also by the simple fact that a group of the disciples had been temporarily left without leadership. The result was that expectations of a miraculous healing were dashed.

The father had expected a cure for his son, who was dumb, deaf, and epileptic. At least those were the symptoms; but the cause was demon-possession. He had brought the boy to the disciples, presuming that that would be as good as bringing him to Jesus himself (17, 18). What is the point of being a disciple of Jesus if you can't pass on his blessings?

Jesus agreed. He too would have expected the disciples to rise to such a challenge. One day they would have to manage without him, and would be left as his representatives in a world full of evil. But for the moment it seems to him that they are no better than the 'faithless generation' around them, and that he stands alone over against everyone else: 'How long am I to be with you?'

The disciples themselves had no doubt expected to be able to cure the boy. They had, after all, done such things before (6:7, 13). But perhaps that was the trouble. They reckoned that the power had been given them, and was thenceforth at their disposal. But 'this kind cannot be driven out by anything but prayer.' ('Fasting' is a thought-provoking addition in some manuscripts, but prayer is the key.) Where they failed, the father succeeded – that is, in a cry for help out of helplessness, which is the essence of the prayer of faith. That is the way to see Jesus work even when he is not with you, dear readers (says Mark). In fact, even before he has done anything the crowd are greatly amazed (15) – he is, quite simply, an amazing person.

TO THINK OVER: What is the point of being a disciple of Jesus if you cannot pass on his blessings?

9:30–37 A calling hard but honourable

From its turning point at Caesarea Philippi, where the messiahship of Jesus was revealed with both its glory and its suffering, Mark's story begins to move steadily towards the cross; and so does the band of disciples, journeying southwards through Galilee. Eight chapters of evidence as to Jesus' identity lead up to the confession of 8:29, and for the next eight those who have grasped who he is will be learning what that means. Both on the road (30) and 'in the house' (33; remember 3:31–35) it is with the disciples that he is now chiefly concerned. Indeed the rest of chapter 9 is a series of loosely connected lessons for them.

And the central lesson? As before, glory to come but humiliation first. To the first prophecy of the cross, at Caesarea Philippi, is now added a second. Verse 31 is plain enough, so the fact that the disciples 'did not understand' means that it was simply too extraordinary for them to take it in. Another explanation is that the actual Aramaic word Jesus used for 'kill' may have been an ambiguous one, like the 'lifted up' in John 12:32; if they thought he was foretelling exaltation, not death, that might account for their arguing about matters of precedence in the coming glory.

They had the grace to be ashamed to admit what they had been talking about. But Jesus knew it anyway, and based an important lesson on it. What makes a man truly great is humility. In Jesus' taking of a child as his illustration, there may be another play on words which we miss, the same Greek word meaning both 'child' and 'servant'. Aim to serve – which means willingness to be put upon, which yet again means the way of suffering.

It is a hard calling. But when he promises that if men receive a child in his name they receive him, for 'child' we can understand 'servant' or 'disciple', and we realise that in that humble role we have the immense honour of being representatives of the Lord himself.

THOUGHT: '...he who receives any one whom I send receives me; and he who receives me receives him who sent me.' (John 13:20).

Questions for further study and discussion on Mark 7:31–9:37

1. What does it mean to talk of Jesus as the Messiah? How does it help us to understand what he came to do? What part should the Old Testament prophecies play in our preaching of Jesus?

2. If God constantly repeats his message in different ways what does that say about our attitude? And what does it suggest about the way we should prepare ourselves, for instance, for Sunday worship?

3. How should we answer people who ask for a sign – be it some miraculous intervention, or some irrefutable proof?

4. We all, at times, miss the deeper spiritual significance of things we read or hear or events in our lives. Share some of your own experiences. What do these teach you? Relate them to Mark 8:14–21.

5. Some Christians seem to believe that to be a Christian is to have no problems and to live constantly with an experience of victory. How do you react – especially in the light of Mark 8:31–35?

6. What special relevance, if any, do you think the account of the transfiguration would have to Christians facing persecution? How would you use it to encourage a Christian in your own country who was going through a difficult time?

7. How does self-confidence show itself in our Christian lives? What are its dangers?

8. What constitutes greatness in our society? How does Jesus' teaching in Mark 9:33–37 challenge this? What are the practical implications for Christians in their place of work and in the church?

9:38–50 A collection of teachings

The rest of the collected sayings which began with verse 33 are linked together less by logic than by word-association.

The first follows the disciples' complaint about an exorcism by a stranger. They were no doubt sore about their own recent failure in this respect (18), and touchy about their special relationship with Jesus (3:14, 15). They did indeed have such a relationship, but it did not mean that they were the only people allowed to do such deeds. Jesus permits this one, calls it a mighty work, and recognises it as done in his name.

Out of the incident he brings the great principle of verse 40. How do men show themselves to be 'for him'? Not only spectacular exorcisms, but even so humble a thing as the giving of a cup of water, if done for his sake, shows that the doer cannot be against Jesus. What matters is not whether the deed is great or small, but whether it is done for him. Perhaps verse 42 takes up verse 37; as Jesus there compared the twelve to children, so now he expresses as much concern for *these* little ones – the exorcist, the water-giver – as for the self-important inner circle.

So to discipleship in general (43–48). 'Hell' here means unquenchable fire, as Mark's footnote in verse 43 translates 'Gehenna'; life means eternal life, explained by making 'kingdom of God' its parallel in verse 47; cutting off one's hand, and so on, means putting a stop to the things your hands do, the ways your feet go, the sights your eyes enjoy, if these betray you into sin.

The fire of hell in the next life (48) leads to the thought of the fire of suffering in this life (49). Some manuscripts explain this saying by adding another: 'Fire, i.e. suffering, is what "salts" Christians (in the sense that salt "salts" sacrifices, i.e. makes them fit to be offered to God).'

Then from the salt of sacrifice we move to salt as a preservative. If Christians, who are meant to affect the world for good, are themselves bad, like second-rate 'salt' which turns out to be full of impurities, which of their worldly neighbours will purify *them*? So, disputatious Christians, behave yourselves!

THOUGHT: What matters is not whether the deed is small or great, but whether it is done for Jesus.

10:1–16 Principles

Marriage, appropriately followed by children – these are the subjects of Jesus' teaching here.

The question about divorce was not so much whether, as when, the law of Moses might allow it. Two noted rabbis differed in their interpretation of Deuteronomy 24:1: Shammai restricted the grounds of divorce; Hillel would permit it for numerous reasons, some quite trivial. The test for Jesus (2) was that, whichever side he took, he would be discredited with the other party.

He, however, aimed to make them think about what was originally *commanded*, not what was subsequently *allowed*. 'Since you break the law anyway, Moses tells you how best to pick up the pieces. But I remind you not of what follows from the law, but of what lies behind it' (5–9). So he goes back to the very start of the 'law of Moses' (Gen. 1:27; 2:24). Indeed his 'let not man put asunder' has a ring of authority about it, quite unlike the scribes' teaching, echoing the great 'let there be' commands of the creation story.

He is, if anything, siding with Shammai, but on such basic principles that no one dares to disagree with him. And on those principles he establishes not only the indissolubility of marriage (9) but the equal responsibility of husband and wife to make it work (11, 12).

What he says about children is similar in tone. They, or those who have brought them, are regarded by the disciples as simply a nuisance. Again Jesus penetrates this thoughtless, superficial attitude to uncover principles beneath. The deepest truth about a child is that it is a model for entry to the kingdom of God. It is mere sentimentality to imagine that he is talking about the child's supposed 'innocence'. What really is true of every child is its helpless dependence: that is the basic qualification for entering the kingdom.

Something else besides the theological question underlies the discussion on divorce. Jesus is in Perea, Herod's territory (1), and his words in verse 12 are a direct comment on the conduct of Herod's wife: for saying the same thing John had been executed (6:17–29). But Jesus is, in any case, on his way to the cross, and in no circumstances now will he mince his words, or teach anything other than plain fundamental truth.

THOUGHT: Surrounded as we are by so much superficial thinking about deep matters, are we prepared to dig for principles?

10:17–27 Life is received, not achieved

It was very unusual to call someone 'good teacher'. Most Jews would have responded as Jesus did in verse 18. This strange verse is actually a key to the whole passage. It is not about the nature of Jesus (saying that he is not God, or not good, or else hinting that he *is* God). Jesus is telling the young man: 'You might use such language less readily if you grasped what real goodness is; and for that you must look to *God*.' That is, we are again directed, as in the previous passage, to fundamental issues.

God's goodness is seen first in the law, which shows us what we ought to *do*. This the questioner understood (17). But then when we discover that such goodness is beyond us, he sends us the gospel, to show us that it is something we have to *receive* as a gift from him (as in v. 15).

General amazement followed Jesus' words on the peril of riches, because wealth was taken to be a sign of blessing. It showed that you must already have achieved God's favour, and it gave you the wherewithal to be generous and thus achieve more of his favour. Yet Jesus calls it a positive hindrance. No wonder the disciples exclaim, 'Then who can be saved?'. The whole basis of acceptance by God was being cut away.

Perhaps the rich man had glimpsed this already. He had achievement, but it seems to have brought him no assurance. So Jesus says, 'If you want eternal life, you must give up *these* things, and follow *me*.' To be able thus to abandon oneself, let alone one's riches, to Jesus is not natural, indeed not possible. His second saying (24) should probably be, not amplified and therefore applicable to fewer people (RSV margin), but simplified and so applicable to more (RSV text). We are *all* incapable of giving up *anything*. Think of the camel and the needle's eye, and don't tone down the idea by saying that 'camel' should be 'rope', as some think, or that the 'needle's eye' was a narrow gateway. The thing is as impossible as getting the biggest creature in Palestine through the smallest opening you can imagine.

FOR PRAYER: Thank God that he can and does do the impossible.

It is hard to deny a glimpse of Little Jack Horner in Peter's words. 'Unlike the rich man (17–22), we have left everything that might earn us eternal life' – as if that leaving would in itself earn them life!

But whatever was in Peter's mind, he has the nub of the matter. The disciples will indeed find life in the age to come, according to Jesus' words to the rich man (17, 21). They have grasped one central truth of the gospel. Now they need to be reminded of another, namely the character of the life of discipleship in the meantime, in this age. On the one hand, there will be renunciation, persecution, and suffering, but on the other hand there will be great compensations. We notice that those who have given up houses *or* brothers *or* sisters will get back far more – houses *and* brothers *and* sisters. Indeed it seems in practice that we realise the fellowship of this new family (compare 3:31–35 again) all the more clearly when times are hard.

So we are once again being shown basic truths: life in this age and what it is like, life in the next age and how it is obtained. The whole thing is upside down by worldly standards (31).

Meanwhile for Jesus also the following of his Father's will means suffering and the loss of all things. For the third time he foretells the cross; here for the first time Jerusalem is indicated as his goal. Following the pattern set in prophecy for the obedience of God's servant, he sets his face like a flint (Isa. 50:5–7). On his carrying out of his Father's will depends everything. Unless he himself leaves all and goes to the cross, there will be no eternal life for anybody.

This picture of Jesus 'leading the way' to the cross is awesome enough. But since the disciples needed reminding about the cross in verse 32b, presumably this was not in their minds in verse 32a. What amazed them therefore was not the Jesus who was inflexibly intent on crucifixion, but Jesus himself as a person – the Jesus who was 'leading' them so authoritatively into these awe-inspiring truths.

THOUGHT: 'Be faithful unto death, and I will give you the crown of life' (Rev. 2:10).

10:35–45 Greatness means service

Again, the disciples betray their gross misunderstanding of Jesus' teaching, as they had done after the previous prediction of the cross (9:30–32). We shall not wonder at their dullness when we remember how easily our own thoughts slip back from the sublime to the foolish. And the conceited request of James and John did arise from a truth, however garbled: they had at least grasped that they would one day be with him in glory. But they had no more idea what they were saying in verse 39, about the cup and the baptism, than they had in verse 37, as Jesus told them. He was speaking of the judgement which awaited him (the cup) and which would overwhelm him (the baptism). In one sense, the fate of the cross was his alone; in another, it would be the lot of all his disciples; but James and John understood neither.

So Jesus gathers the whole group – the rest, indignant because James and John had got in first, were no better – and patiently takes them back once more to the principles.

For again it is the reversal of worldly values they have to learn. As with dying or living (8:35), being last or first (9:35; 10:31), being poor or rich (10:21, 29, 30), so now in the matter of greatness or humiliation the truth is the opposite of what the world thinks. Values 'among you', the people of God, must be the opposite of those held by the Gentiles, meaning all who do not belong to his people.

In this particular reversal the pattern of greatness is to be Jesus himself, who though he is Lord is also Servant – in fact the latter qualifies him to be the former (Phil. 2:7, 9, 11). Jesus in turn follows the pattern of the Servant in Isaiah 53. The cross has the same double meaning when regarded as Jesus' service as it did when thought of as his cup and his baptism. In one sense it is unique: only he could die 'as a ransom for many'. Yet it is also an example: we are to be prepared for the humiliation of service, because he came to serve (45).

TO THINK OVER: How do mistaken ideas of greatness show themselves in the church today?

10:46–52 Blind Bartimaeus meets the Messiah

As he leaves the ancient city of Jericho – perhaps as he approaches the new Roman city built by Herod just to the south of it, which would account for Luke 18:35 – Jesus comes, not within sight, but at any rate within earshot, of the blind beggar known simply as the son of Timaeus. Thus Mark translates the Aramaic *Bar-Timai* for the benefit of his non-Jewish readers.

But in fact the whole incident has important Jewish background which is worth noting. Although Bartimaeus' cry 'Son of David', for instance, does not necessarily mean that the beggar belived Jesus to be the coming messianic king, Mark's readers will, with hindsight, certainly read that meaning back into it. Once Jesus is recognised as Messiah, such a title is seen to be altogether apt, and all the circumstances fit into place. The messianic claim is not now to be hushed up, as it was in 8:30, for Jesus is on his way to declare himself publicly at the gates of Jerusalem. Perhaps the throwing aside of Bartimaeus' cloak means that it had been spread open before him to receive alms. If so, the coming of Messiah will do away with the necessity of begging. Having shown his faith by his persistence, he is then encouraged to put his desire into words, always a helpful practice in bringing our needs to the Lord. And he is duly healed. Both the 'taking heart' and the healing (49, 52) figure in prophecies of the coming Messiah (e.g. Isa. 35:4, 5). It is as though Mark is putting together the essential components of the picture. He has already said that there will indeed be glory, but there must first be a cross; then, that while this means self-sacrifice on Jesus' part, it will require similar sacrifice from the disciples as well; now he reminds them of what they had earlier seen but could have forgotten – that Messiah's coming will in the end (and also on the way!) bring healing, salvation, and joy.

Bartimaeus is thus in several respects a model of discipleship. Till Jesus came, he had sat useless beside the way; now he can follow him on it (46, 52). That is, he joins the pilgrims as they go up to Jerusalem, praising God for what he has been enabled to see.

TO THINK OVER: If the coming of the Messiah has done away with the necessity for begging, what responsibility does the church, the community of the Messiah, have for the poor?

11:1–11 The arrival at Jerusalem

Detailed preparation lies behind the events of Palm Sunday. In the practical sense, arrangements seem to have been made in advance for the borrowing of the colt. It might even be that what the disciples were told to say to questioners was, '*The owner* needs it and will be returning it at once,' the owner being with Jesus' company at the time.

In another sense, prophecy had long ago prepared for this great day. The outstanding reference is Zechariah 9:9, which speaks of the coming of Zion's king, his riding on an ass, and the city's rejoicing. Zechariah had also spoken (14:1–9) of the revealing of Messiah's glory on the Mount of Olives; and although that belongs to the end of the age, this was a prefiguring of it.

Other Old Testament Scriptures may well have come to the minds of some who witnessed these events. Psalm 118:25, 26 was actually quoted: 'Blessed is he who comes in the name of the Lord.' 'He who comes' might also be the mysterious person of Genesis 49:10, especially since that passage goes on to mention his tied colt, and Mark seems at pains to note the untying of the animal. Furthermore, animals which had not been put to ordinary use were especially appropriate for a special use of this kind (e.g. Deut. 21:3; 1 Sam. 6:7).

In spite of all this, the fulfilling of Scripture was still not so incontrovertible that people *had* to believe it. 'Blessed is he who comes,' certainly, and 'Blessed is the kingdom,' but the first might mean any pilgrim, and even if it meant Jesus it did not necessarily mean that the two were one and that Jesus embodied the kingdom. Although Zechariah 9:9 was coming true before their eyes, his enemies were not forced to accept the fact.

Before such truths could be seen and accepted, a supernatural eye-opening was required, corresponding to that which Bartimaeus had just been given at Jericho. Only as we beg that from the Son of David will each event stand out in this new light, and our Hosanna be not merely a cheerful noise but a cry to the Lord who is bringing us salvation. Otherwise Palm Sunday ends in anticlimax; the enthusiasm evaporates and the crowds go home.

THOUGHT: Join today in the song of praise to the One who brings salvation.

11:12–21 The Lord comes to his Temple

There is one quotation (Isa. 56:7) and one allusion (Jer. 7:11) in this passage (17), but Jesus' cleansing of the Temple has a great deal more Old Testament background than that. Behind the trading lay the need to provide pilgrims with the right coins for the Temple tax and the right animals for sacrifice. But it was the Court of the Gentiles that was being used for this, and behind Jesus' anger was the fact that Gentiles in particular were thus being hindered from worshipping God, in spite of the frequent call of the prophets that 'all the nations' should be able to come to him. As before, the words of Zechariah (14:16–21) seem to be much in Jesus' mind.

On either side of this incident (another of Mark's sandwiches, compare 5:21–43) are placed the two halves of the story of the fig-tree. Some disapprove of the violence of verse 15, or presume bad temper in verse 14. But do not these two unexpected displays of emotion shed light on each other? Mark almost seems to say: 'The disciples heard Jesus' words to the *tree*, bore them in mind while the corresponding event took place in the *Temple*, and then came back to the *tree* and found that its case was indeed hopeless.' For the two facts, that 'he was hungry' (12) and that 'it was not the season for figs' (13), combined to provide Jesus with an acted parable for his disciples about the fruitlessness of another 'tree' from which he looked for results. For the fig-tree represents Israel. At his coming he should have found the blessings of Israel being made available to all nations; and it was not so.

Mark has not recorded the relevant words of Matthew 21:43, but he does note that Jesus was later accused of threatening to replace the Temple with 'another, not made with hands' (14:58). There would soon come into existence a tree which *would* bear fruit, a temple which *would* be open to all nations, namely the Christian church. Does it? Is it? Members of the new Israel may need to remind themselves today, when society mixes people of many different backgrounds and cultures, of the kind of fruitlessness for which the old Israel was condemned.

TO THINK OVER: '...a great multitude which no man could number, from every nation, from all the tribes and peoples and tongues, standing... before the Lamb...' (Rev. 7:9)

Questions for further study and discussion on Mark 9:38–11:21

1. What factors, today, hinder the acceptance of others who claim to be acting in the name of Jesus? How should we act on the principles of Mark 9:38–41?

2. Discuss the different qualities and uses of salt. Why is it an appropriate symbol for the Christian? How is your church acting as salt in your community?

3. Why is 'helpless dependence the basic qualification for entering the kingdom' (note on Mark 10:1–16)? How does the story of Mark 10:17–22 illustrate this? In what ways might this make it hard for modern men and women to become Christians?

4. What are the dangers of riches? Bearing in mind that most of us, in world terms at least, are rich, what does this say to us?

5. What has this section of Mark's Gospel taught you about Christian leadership?

6. On the basis of these chapters how would you define 'worldliness'? And what is the Christian's attitude to it?

7. What place does Jesus' entry into Jerusalem play in the developing picture of his role as Messiah? What would you see as its chief significance for today?

8. The comments on 11:12–21 refer to the church being open to all. What different cultures and backgrounds are present in your community? What is your church doing to reach them? What more could you do?

11:22–33 Great things are happening

We broke off, and have now begun again, in the middle of a paragraph. 'Jesus answered' Peter's realisation that judgement had fallen on the fruitless fig-tree by going straight on to talk about faith, prayer, and forgiveness; so Mark represents the sequence of events.

Although it is not easy to see, he presumably makes a connection between divine judgement on the tree (and Jesus' anger in the Temple, which was related) and divine answers to prayer. It was certainly the power and authority of God that the disciples had just witnessed in both incidents. Is the connection that when we pray with undoubting faith (24) and with forgiving hearts (25), we shall receive not simply answers, but answers which are in some way like those recent happenings?

If so, we should note three things. Jesus' actions with regard to the tree and the Temple were clearly to do with the fact that God was visiting his people. Messiah was present and active as the Scripture had said he would be. To pray in faith is to align ourselves with what Scripture tells us is his purpose and plan.

Secondly, the casting of a mountain into the sea may be more than simply a vivid example of the impossibilities which believing prayer can achieve. The mountain may be Olivet, where they were standing, and the sea may be the Dead Sea, visible from it; and the words may be meant to recall once more the words of Zechariah – not just Zechariah 4:7, but the levelling of that very land, which the prophet spoke of as one of the mighty events of the Day of the Lord (Zech. 14:4, 5, 10). Are our prayers 'waiting for and hastening the coming of' that day (2 Pet. 3:12)?

Thirdly, the Jewish leaders, out to trap Jesus yet again, are again hoist with their own petard. They must know in their hearts that John the Baptist had divine authority. But if they admit that, they will have to admit that Jesus has the same authority – that the things they are witnessing are the acts of Messiah, and that the Day of the Lord has in a sense already begun. Such acts (and Scripture teaches what they can be) we can with confidence claim from God in prayer.

THOUGHT: To pray in faith is to align ourselves with what Scripture tells us is God's purpose and plan.

12:1–12 The rebellious tenants

Compared with earlier parables, this one has new and disturbing features. For one thing, it looks in some ways more like an allegory; its descriptive items (hedge, winepress, tower, etc) – is each supposed to 'stand for' something? The vineyard's owner is God, the son is Jesus, and the tenants are the Jewish leaders. But the details cannot all fit. The fond hopes of verse 6 may be the owner's, but they are surely not God's. Neither would the chief priests have assumed what the tenants presumably did – that since the heir had come, the owner must have died, so that if the son died too they could legally claim the vineyard. No; this is a true parable, with one main point. The details simply set the scene, even though more of them than usual turn out in allegorical manner to fit the facts.

The scene they set is a typical Galilean estate, with its absentee landlord requiring rent in kind. But Mark makes another of his sandwiches by framing the story between two references (1, 9) to Isaiah 5:1–7. He shows Jesus departing from his usual custom; for speaking to the Jewish leaders, he utters the parable explicitly 'against them' (12), since they know that the vineyard in Isaiah 5 means Israel.

They draw the obvious conclusion; and this too is a new development. Still Jesus has made no unequivocal claims about himself. Verse 9 might be taken to refer merely to the owner, not to God, and the owner's son might be thought to mean simply the last messenger, and not necessarily the Son of God. But it is increasingly hard even for the wilfully blind enemies of Jesus to miss the implication of what he is saying, especially when he underlines it with yet another Scripture (Ps. 118:22, 23). 'They perceived' at last a gleam of the truth, and it strengthened their determination not to accept it. Eduard Schweizer points out that for Mark a parable is not an illustration to help us understand spiritual truth, but 'a way of speaking about God, to which a mere intellectual response is not possible. The only person who can understand a parable is one who is willing to accept or reject its message.' The parable-teller says bluntly to his hearers (and readers), 'If the cap fits, wear it.'

THOUGHT: 'If any man's will is to do his will, he shall know whether the teaching is from God' (John 7:17).

12:13–17 The question about Roman taxes

By this, the first of a series of questions to Jesus, the plot against him is further advanced. The questioners' hypocrisy (15) is obvious as soon as they open their mouths: the very compliments they pay are designed to force Jesus to commit himself one way or the other – to forfeit his popular support by approving of Roman taxes, or to risk official condemnation by disapproving of them. Those who supported Herod, who ruled with Roman backing, naturally upheld the system, while the Pharisees, though they accepted it, resented it. But they are prepared to make common cause against Jesus, no longer simply to test him (8:11, 10:2), but now actually to entrap him (13).

By his answer, however, not only is the plot foiled for the time being, but his reputation is further enhanced. He says in effect: 'The picture and the inscription on this coin are Caesar's; so since you are prepared to use it' (they have had no difficulty in producing it!) 'you are recognising that the coinage itself belongs to him. Whatever you reckon is due to him, that you must pay to him.' Thus he throws the question back to them, together with the responsibility for working out its implications. They who meant to entrap him are themselves entrapped. 'His talk', far from betraying him, amazes them (13, 17).

But he says more than this. In his reply, disciples (and readers) are further instructed. He speaks of what is Caesar's in the context of what is God's. Caesar has a place in God's world, and some things do belong to him. What is due to him, we pay. Here in embryo is the doctrine of the state, to be amplified in such passages as Romans 13:1–7. But God has his rights also, and they are paramount. By adding the second half of his reply (17), Jesus is saying, 'Your question left out the vital matter of *ultimate* authority.' The rule of the state is there for our benefit, but we are not to regard it uncritically, especially when its coinage, so to speak, begins to bear the word 'divine' – when, that is, it begins to direct our lives in ways that deviate from 'the way of God' (14).

TO THINK OVER: How might government legislation direct our lives in ways that deviate from 'the way of God'?

12:18–27 The question about the resurrection

Here for the first time in Mark the Sadducees appear. Being the 'establishment', a priestly aristocracy which collaborated with the Roman government, they would have been as concerned as the Pharisees to silence Jesus. Their question seems designed, however, not to trap him but merely to ridicule him – and that in a matter in which both people and Pharisees would have sided with him. Perhaps we are meant to see less his escape from a series of snares than his supremacy in every encounter, whatever its motive.

The question has two aspects. First, it was ostensibly about marriage. The principle of 'levirate' marriage, which the Sadducees' example illustrates, was, as they said, part of the Mosaic law (Deut. 25:5–10). But the question was really about resurrection. They sat loose to all Scripture except the law of Moses, and even that they interpreted in a rationalistic way: 'We can't believe the *fact* of resurrection, and we're sure that Moses didn't either, because levirate marriage (to take only one item of his teaching) would make the *manner* of it so ridiculous.'

This leads directly to the two aspects of Jesus' answer. He says they are quite simply wrong: wrong as to the manner of the resurrection, because they do not know the power of God, and as to the fact of it, because they do not know the Scripture. Beyond this world God's power has brought into being another, where life is like that of the angels (something else the Sadducees don't believe in!) – life without end, service without pain, love without limit. Relationships of a depth which for us is restricted to marriage will there be known universally, without restriction. And as to the fact of the resurrection, Jesus turns to this same Moses whom they have used to discredit the idea, and refers them to 'the passage about the bush' (Exod. 3:6). In effect, he says: 'God here reminds Moses that he made a covenant with the patriarchs, and though they had long been dead, that covenant guaranteed that the ever-living God would *never* let them down. It is inconceivable, therefore, that any enemy, even the last enemy, death, could break their relationship with him: so he rightly says not "I was", but "I am" their God. Because he is alive now, they also must be.'

THOUGHT: 'God himself will be with them; he will wipe away every tear from their eyes, and death shall be no more, neither shall there be mourning nor crying nor pain any more...' (Rev. 21:3, 4).

12:28–37 The two last questions

The question of the Pharisees and the Herodians arose from ill-will, that of the Sadducees from unbelief. By contrast, the scribe's has every appearance of sincerity. In reply, Jesus quotes Deuteronomy 6:5 and Leviticus 19:18. He includes the preface to the first of these – 'Hear, O Israel: the *Lord*' – reminding his hearers that God has spoken to them, loved them, and made them his covenant people; for that is the meaning of his name *YHWH*, the Lord. What therefore is asked of them is their devotion to him, in a personal relationship of love, responding to his covenant grace. All other laws are not things we must do to gain his approval, but simply aspects of that response. Thus the scribe, though he did not ask for it, is given a second commandment as a corollary to the first, since loving God means that we shall want to regard everything and everyone else as he regards them.

Jesus' questioners being silenced, the remaining question is one put to them by him. He raises an issue as central as that just raised by the scribe, whose question basically concerned the relationship between God and man. Jesus takes the same crucial matter one step further, to the means by which that relationship is made possible: he re-focuses attention on himself as Messiah and Redeemer.

The Scripture he now quotes (Ps. 110) was recognised as one dealing with the Messiah. In what sense do the scribes speak of Messiah as David's son? Like most Jews, they see him as a descendant of David's, on David's throne, with the same kind of power as David's; in other words a political king. But in David's prophetic vision, his great descendant is called his lord, *adonai* (not *YHWH* – the name of him who speaks at the start of the quotation – but still a remarkable title), and is enthroned not in Jerusalem but at God's right hand on high. Messiah's victories will be of a loftier order than David's, primarily spiritual, not political, and will make available to all men the relationship with God spoken of at the start of our passage. No wonder 'the great throng heard him gladly' (37).

CHALLENGE: '…with all your heart, and with all your soul, and with all your mind, and with all your strength.'

12:38–44 Outward show, inward devotion

Mark does not add these closing verses simply because of a superficial association of ideas (as if scribes in v. 35 remind him of v. 38, and widows in v. 40 remind him of v. 42). All the questions of this chapter are essentially about God, what he says, and what he really requires. In teaching Scripture, the scribes held a key position. This was generally accepted, and they were honoured for it. They were distinguished by their dress, and were the objects of public respect and private beneficence. Christians similarly are exhorted to honour those who minister the word of God (1 Tim. 5:17).

But, with exceptions such as the questioner of verses 28–34, most Jewish scribes fell into the obvious danger and under the condemnation of Jesus. How easy it was for them to begin to *desire* respect and distinction, and to 'sponge on the hospitality of people of limited means', as W.L. Lane paraphrases verse 40a! And how ironic that those who are immersed in the teachings of Scripture, which are designed to fix the heart upon God, should in that very occupation become so concerned about the praise of men and the satisfaction of self! It is because their calling is so honourable that they merit 'the greater condemnation'.

On his way out of the Temple Jesus stops by the great trumpet-shaped collecting boxes, and there sees someone who provides him with a perfect contrast to the scribes and a summary of all he has been saying. A woman puts into the treasury two *lepta* (the equivalent of one *quadrans*, your smallest coin, explains Mark in a footnote to his Roman readers). Somehow, whether supernaturally or otherwise, Jesus knows both that she is a widow and that this is all the money she possesses. The lesson for his disciples is that the amount of one's giving is not the important thing. What matters far more is, how much it represents of one's total wealth; or, if you like, how much one has left. Behind that is the absolutely basic question, which underlies also all the discussions of this chapter, which causes the widow to stand out in such contrast to the scribes, and which we have to ask ourselves: how totally am I devoted and submitted to God, his truth, his word, and his demands?

THOUGHT: What matters is not the amount of our giving: it is how much we have left.

Questions for further study and discussion on Mark 11:22–12:44

1. It is often said that our prayers are not answered because we lack faith. How far is this supported by Mark 11:20–25? What other reasons might these verses suggest?

2. If the acts of Jesus indicated that Messiah has come and the Day of the Lord has begun, what acts should we expect to see today to demonstrate that truth? Does this suggest any changes in our church life?

3. Look back over some of Mark's parables and see how they illustrate Schweizer's comment, 'The only person who can understand a parable is one who is willing to accept or reject its message.' (See comments on Mark 12:1–12.)

4. Most people begrudge paying taxes. What should the Christian attitude be? How far should we try to influence the ways in which they are spent? Discuss ways of doing this.

5. What ideas do people today have about heaven? What ideas has the church had? How far do these ideas reflect the sort of life that Jesus hints at in Mark 12:24–27? Compare this with other Scriptures.

6. What is the relationship between the 'first and second' commandments of 12:28–31? Can we effectively observe either one without the other? Is the measure of our observance of the second a right way of testing our observance of the first?

7. How far should the widow of 12:41–44 become an example for us to follow? What principles should govern our giving? Is there anything more that your church could do to ensure right attitudes on the part of the members?

8. How should we care for those who teach?

13:1–13 What is to come – I

The disciples may not have been altogether taken aback at Jesus' prophecy of the Temple's doom. His earlier quotation about its being a den of robbers (11:17; Jer. 7:11) may have reminded them that that prophecy goes on to speak, like many others, of judgement on the city of God.

At any rate, the discourse which takes up this whole chapter, perhaps the most difficult in the Gospel, is a re-statement on the grand scale of the now familiar theme of 'tribulation before glory'. Immediately impending is the passion of Jesus; at the far end of the vision which he opens up for them is his glorious return. As his own earthly ministry is about to end, he prepares to launch his church on its ministry, giving to the same four original disciples the encouragement they need for the troubled times ahead.

For that is the object of Mark 13. All the complex and often misunderstood events that it foresees are simply the background to, and the reason for, a series of thoroughly practical instructions. Here is the concern of the shepherd for his flock. Jesus has a word for his disciples' confused minds (5) and troubled hearts (7), and exhortations and warnings of this kind are the points we shall find him repeating again and again throughout the chapter. Whatever they meant by 'these things' (4), he shifts the focus of attention away from the destruction of the Temple to 'the end' of all things, and his first warning is that events which might look like signs of the end in fact are not. They are only the beginning, that is, if they signify anything, it is 'more to follow'! As well as wars and famines, there will be suffering, betrayal, and death at the hands of authorities both religious and secular (9–13). But the power of God's Spirit will be with his people, and although what is promised them is not rescue, but only the right words to say, yet the great object – testimony for the sake of Jesus – will be achieved. There is a 'must' about the proclamation of the gospel (10), as there was about the troubles of the world (7), which, however dismaying the prospect, comforts us with the reminder that God is working his purpose out and is ultimately in control.

QUESTION: In what situations do we have the right to believe that verse 11 might apply to us?

13:14–27 What is to come – II

The disciples' confused picture of what is to come is separated out by Jesus into three main areas: the destruction of Jerusalem, the second coming, and the church age as a whole. As we have already seen, his prime concern is with the third – with how his church can be prepared for whatever may happen. He has spoken in this general way from verse 5 to verse 13.

Now he goes on to speak particularly of the destruction of Jerusalem, which was the original question. The 'desolating sacrilege' was a fearful event prophesied in Daniel (e.g. 11:31). Some thought it happened in 168 BC, when Antiochus IV desecrated the Temple by sacrificing a pig to Zeus. Caligula's proposed setting up of an image there in AD 40 would have been a similar outrage. But the real fulfilment came with the war of AD 66–70 and the Temple's desecration by both Jewish Zealots and Romans in turn, in the war which ended with the sack of the city. Many saw in time that Jerusalem, for centuries a refuge to flee *to*, had become at last a place to flee *from*. Certainly there were Christians who escaped before the final siege to the city of Pella in Transjordan, heeding Jesus' prophetic warning.

The events of AD 70 were an unparalleled disaster (19), not only because of the terrible suffering involved, but because in one sense they wrote *finis* to the story of Israel, and the first half of history came to an end. The people of God would no longer be identical with the Israelite nation or the descendants of Abraham. All this is set in the context of Jesus' loving care for his church, a concern that it should not sit passively assuming that the second coming was about to happen, but should take the obvious practical steps to escape while it could. For not even this catastrophe, let alone the wars and famines and earthquakes of verses 7, 8, would be a sign of the end. That would not come till afterwards. In verse 24 we should stress not 'In *those* days', that is the same days as in verse 19, as if Jesus meant the second coming would quickly follow the fall of Jerusalem, but rather 'the days *after* that tribulation', i.e. his return belongs to a later period than the one just described.

THOUGHT: Whenever Jesus' return may come, we are to serve him while we may and suffer for him when we must.

13:28–37 What is to come – III

One possible interpretation of this much-debated passage is represented by the following summary of the whole discourse, starting again from the disciples' question in verse 4 about 'the sign when these things' (the destruction of the Temple, v. 2) 'are all to be accomplished'. (Note, when we reach v. 29, that 'he' in that verse could equally well be translated 'it').

Verses 5–13: 'I want to tell you about the end of the world, as well as about the destruction of the Temple. Many things will happen which you will be tempted to think are signs of the end. You will be wrong; they are simply constantly-recurring features of the church age.' *Verses 14–23*: 'Referring to your original question, Jerusalem will indeed be sacked; but even that disaster will not be the end, nor even a sign of it (21).' *Verses 24–27*: 'By contrast, when the end really does come it will be quite unmistakable (26), a cataclysm beside which even the sack of Jerusalem will seem trivial.'

In the two remaining paragraphs, which make up today's passage, Jesus takes up in the same order the same two topics just dealt with: Jerusalem, and the end. Now however he ties up the whole matter by finally answering the query about signs (4). *Verses 28–31*: 'These things (29), the events relating to the desolating sacrilege, will indicate that *it* – the destruction of Jerusalem – is near. Think of the fig-tree, which *does* give signs of what is coming (unlike the householder – see below). Some of this generation will still be living, will see the sacrilege in the Temple, and will flee, for that will be the sign when these things are all to be accomplished (4).' *Verses 32–37*: 'But *that* day (32), the end of the world, will be different. Think of the householder who goes away and *does not* give warning of when he is about to return. So with regard to the end, the Master's return, you are to watch not for preliminary signs, but simply for the return itself, and be ready.'

What Jesus stresses throughout is the practical matter of our preparedness for his own second coming, and for whatever may come our way in the meantime. Notice where he pins our attention by the four occurrences of the phrase 'Take heed' in this chapter (5, 9, 23, 33).

THOUGHT: 'You are not in darkness ... for that day to surprise you like a thief. For you are all ... sons of the day ... So then let us not sleep, as others do, but let us keep awake and be sober' (1 Thess. 5:4–6).

14:1–11 How much is Jesus worth?

'Two days before the Passover' begins Mark's story of the Passion. So it is a sequence of actual historical events which can be anchored in the calendar, and which are filled with meaning by the background to that Jewish festival. The leaders seek to arrest Jesus: no easy matter in view of his fame, the huge crowds in Jerusalem, the Passover theme of deliverance from oppressors, and therefore the risk of popular insurrection and Roman retaliation. Judas seeks a chance to betray him, perhaps in line with an official 'Wanted' notice that has been published (John 11:57).

The incident at Bethany is another thing altogether. If it is the one described in John 12:1–8, it had happened a few days earlier. But Mark, framing it between the two 'seekings' (1, 11), contrasts the ways in which hate and love express themselves. The fact that a denarius was a day's wage (Matt. 20:2) gives us some idea of the value of the ointment which the woman 'wasted' on Jesus. The churlish objection of verse 5 is in John 12 attributed to Judas; contrast the thirty pieces of silver (Matt. 26:15) that he was prepared to take (not to give!) for Jesus. But his words are the opportunity for the breathtaking insight of verses 6–9. The cross is as far as the enemies of Jesus can see. But he, as he looks ahead, sees his death, his burial, his resurrection – for how can there be a gospel without a resurrection? – and the universal spread of that gospel. And an integral part of it will be the story of how this woman valued Jesus. For her gift *was* 'given to the poor' (5). Scripture sets before us 'the Poor Man' as a picture of one helpless and humiliated, unjustly persecuted, friendless and forsaken, whose hope is in God alone. To see Jesus in that picture, and to honour and love him for it, is to be very near the heart of the gospel. The fact that we always have the poor with us (7) is not an excuse for doing nothing about economic injustice; but neither is it a reason for exalting the second great commandment above the first. More important than concern for our fellow man is worship of our Lord – worth-ship, the expression of how much we think he is worth.

TO THINK OVER: What spontaneous, and costly, ways do we have of showing our devotion?

Whether the supper took place on or before Passover night is an unsolved problem, debated at length in the commentaries. Matthew, Mark, and Luke seem to indicate the one, John the other. Suffice it to say that we are clearly meant to regard it as a Passover meal. For once, Mark does not attempt to explain the Jewish technicalities to his Gentile readers, but simply fastens on two or three points. The dipping of bread in the dish of sauce turns our thoughts directly to the cross, for it is at this point that Jesus reveals that there is a traitor among the twelve. So this passage, like the previous one, ends in the sombre shadow of betrayal (11, 21, and on to 42).

But that is not where it began. Again, the treachery of Judas is set in the wider context of an overruling plan. All has been prepared beforehand. On a simple practical level, plans for the supper have been made in advance (as with the arrival in Jerusalem in 11:2–10). The unusual sight of a man with a water-jar must be a pre-arranged sign, and the householder has ready what Jesus knows will be 'a large upper room furnished'. The betrayal falls into place against a biblical background also. If Psalm 41:1, 2 was in mind with the woman at Bethany who 'considered' Jesus, and so was 'called blessed in the land', verses 9, 10 are even more apt with regard to Judas: 'Even my bosom friend in whom I trusted, who ate of my bread, has lifted his heel against me.' Nor is it only individual stages in the whole tragic yet glorious process which have been mapped out beforehand. The entire 'going' of the Son of man is taking place 'as it is written' (21).

It is clear that Judas cannot on that account claim diminished responsibility. What he does, he does deliberately, or Jesus would not declare 'woe' to him. The doctrine of predestination is not an excuse for any of us to say 'I couldn't help myself.' Yet the paradox is that all is nevertheless within the plan and under the controlling hand of the God who will use even the wrath of man in the redeeming of his people, as he did long before on the first Passover night.

THOUGHT: 'Jesus, delivered up according to the definite plan and foreknowledge of God, you crucified and killed by the hands of lawless men' (Acts 2:23).

14:22-31 The last supper – II

After the dipping in the dish, the other point in the Passover meal at which Mark lingers is the thanksgiving for and sharing of the bread and the cup. He does not explain which bread, or which of the four cups, in the complex ritual. Even Paul's comments on the Lord's Supper (and he says little enough about it) contain more than this brief account of its institution. They also illuminate it by showing how the early church understood it.

The shared elements mean first the unity of the Lord's people with him and with one another (1 Cor. 10:16, 17). We may imagine the disciples' astonishment as Jesus introduced startling new words into the time-honoured liturgy. Their minds were torn away from the 'bread of affliction' which related to the old deliverance from Egypt, and the cup now represented a covenant of a new kind which would replace the covenant of Sinai. Through the body and blood of Jesus a new thing was coming into being of the same kind as, but infinitely greater than, the nation founded at the Exodus. A new Israel was being established.

The supper means secondly a proclamation of Jesus' death, to be repeated until his second coming (1 Cor. 11:26). First death then glory: the inexorable theme of Mark, the Gospel of the Servant, sounds yet again. The history of the new people of God begins with Jesus' suffering and will end with his return. This too is here in the original words. The immediate tragedy is the pouring out of the blood (24). The ultimate glory will be when at last the feast of victory reunites him and all his people in heaven (25).

Do the disciples need yet another illustration of this principle? They are given it at once: within three days they will experience *both* the death of their leader and the breaking of their fellowship, *and* his rising and their reunion (27, 28). But it is so hard to grasp! Well, let them, and all who like them find the way of Jesus a way of pain, remember these words from the last of the six psalms they will have sung before setting out for Gethsemane: 'I shall not die, but I shall live, and recount the deeds of the Lord' (Ps. 118:17).

QUESTION: Do we allow a note of victory into our celebrations of the Lord's Supper?

14:32–42 Abba, Father

Mark does not bother to translate Gethsemane (oil-press); that is simply the name of an olive garden. Abba is a different matter. He wants us to know both that Abba means Father, and that although most Jews would have thought this a gross over-familiarity, it was Jesus' word for his Father God. We likewise find we can be equally 'familiar' with God (Rom. 8:15–17).

To Abba Jesus turns in his extremity. As from the start of his ministry he had felt the need to go 'out to a lonely place' to pray (1:35), so now at its climax he finds a little 'wilderness' where he can be away from distraction and see things clearly by drawing closer to his Father.

It is to Abba and not to his remaining eleven disciples that he turns for strengthening. As he had left the city, so he left both the eight, and then even the three, knowing that none of them could be relied on (27). Peter, James, and John were taken farthest with him, but that was for their sake, not his. These three self-important men (10:37; 14:29) needed to learn the way of the suffering Servant (10:45). 'Watch and pray', not to keep me company, but to keep yourselves from temptation (38).

To Abba Jesus comes at the end of all things, knowing that what prayer achieves is the aligning of our wills with our Father's will, and that our truest joy lies in this. What, then, if that will turns out to be the 'cup', the hour of suffering which will not go away (35, 36), and which is no ordinary suffering, but the wrath of God against sin? What if at the time of greatest need a son flees for refuge to his dearly loved father, and finds that Abba's will is *this*? – that the way of the privileged Son has to be the way of the submissive Servant? Perhaps already, in his sorrow 'even to death', Jesus can hear the pre-echo of his own cry of dereliction on the cross (15:34). 'The only answer Jesus receives to his prayer is the hard answer of events', beginning 'with the failure of the three to watch with him' (C.E.B. Cranfield).

THOUGHT: This *is* our Abba: he *does* love us, though his blessings can come to us in no other way.

14:43–52 The arrest

With the arrival of the party come to arrest Jesus, we come to the core of the passion story, the heart of what the early church believed and preached.

To his irredeemable wickedness Judas adds the sin of hypocrisy, with an action that says 'Respect and love' and means just the opposite. Then he disappears from Mark's story, having, ironically, set the tone for all that is to follow: 'The one I shall kiss is the man.' For Jesus now dominates the scene, even more, if it were possible, than on any earlier occasion. All focuses on him. This is the man whom these very guards have known as a teacher of righteousness, preaching constantly in the Temple unmolested as they themselves patrolled it, one they know does not deserve arrest. This is the man who is now nevertheless assailed as if he were a robber, so that the prophetic words of Isaiah 53:12 begin to come true in him, 'He ... was numbered with the transgressors.' This is the man who now stands isolated, again fulfilling prophecy both ancient and recent (27; Zech. 13:7). Even his friends fail to understand him, thinking to prevent by the sword the fulfilling of his destiny (poor Peter again, though only John, writing much later, tells us it was he), and then desert him altogether.

So it is Jesus alone upon whom all this suffering is to fall. And as if to stamp as factual truth the narrative which here begins this central story which all the church of Christ holds to be of prime importance (1 Cor. 15:3–8), Mark adds a personal signature: 'I was there'. Commentators find it very hard to account for verses 51, 52 if the young man was *not* Mark, risen from bed in his home in Jerusalem, perhaps the very house where the supper had just taken place (14:15; Acts 1:13; 12:12), and throwing a sheet or loose garment around himself to follow Jesus and the eleven. 'I was no more courageous than the rest,' he says, 'but at least I saw it happen.'

THOUGHT: Every re-reading of the gospel story should impress on us afresh, in mind, imagination, emotions, and spirit, the conviction that at the centre of it is the passion of our Lord, and that for our sake he really did suffer and die.

Questions for further study and discussion on Mark 13:1–14:52

1. What is your reaction to interpretations of prophecy that major on specific links between prophetic details and modern developments in political and military areas? Do you think they adequately reflect the intention of Jesus in Mark 13?

2. What help does Jesus' teaching in Mark 13 give us in developing a Christian attitude to war, civil unrest and natural disasters?

3. Jesus encouraged his followers to leave Jerusalem and go to some place of safety. When might it be right, and when wrong, to run away from troubled situations? What guidelines are there here for Christians in areas of political disturbance today?

4. What justification, if any, do Christians have for looking for signs of the end?

5. By economic or even humanitarian standards the action of the woman in 14:3–9 is senseless, but what is its spiritual worth? What does this teach about the values by which we should live?

6. What important truths were communicated through the Last Supper? How effectively are they communicated through the observance of the Lord's Supper in your church? What would you like to see changed?

7. We are called to 'share the fellowship of his sufferings'. Discuss what this might involve in the light of the incidents in Gethsemane.

8. Why did Jesus so value 'the lonely place'? What place do we give to prayer in our own lives? How important is it to get away from the influence of others?

14:53–65 On oath before the Sanhedrin

What an unlikely scene! In the dead of night, in so respectable a house as the high priest's, an upstairs room with a host of eminent people hastily assembled, and a courtyard below with a fire lit, servants still up, a crowd of guards waiting. Mark will tell us later (66–72) what happens to Peter in the courtyard; upstairs the scene is dominated again by Jesus.

At first he is dominant even in his silence. Commentators differ over the legality of this trial, indeed over whether it was a trial at all, or simply a preliminary enquiry to find proper grounds for a charge against Jesus. Around him is the ebb and flow of conflicting evidence brought by a whole series of witnesses, which from the point of view of the high priest (Caiaphas, Matt. 26:57) turns out to be no more than a maddening waste of time. Still Jesus stands silent as the damaging report about a threatened destruction of the Temple is brought (compare John 2:19). Perhaps it is the messianic overtones of this charge, the failure of all the others, and the desire to speed things up, which decide Caiaphas to fasten on the matter of Jesus' supposed messiahship and to force him on oath to answer. So at last Jesus speaks; and in none of Mark's scenes is attention so riveted on him as with the sensational 'I am' of verse 62.

His blasphemy (64) is that he dishonours God by claiming to be God's chosen Messiah when anyone can see he isn't. Whatever people may have thought of his feeding 5,000, or riding into Jerusalem, or teaching magisterially in the Temple, even those possible indications of greatness count for nothing now. And it is at this point, as a friendless, helpless prisoner, that he at last makes the great claim unequivocally, and the secret is out.

To the Jewish leaders, his humiliation is the proof that he cannot be Messiah. And that is *their* blasphemy. Because Mark is the Gospel of the Servant; it is precisely there, in his humiliation, that the true Servant of God should be recognised. Yet again Mark's readers are to learn from their Lord that to serve and to suffer are the prime characteristics both of him and of those who follow him.

THOUGHT: 'Being found in human form he humbled himself... Therefore God has highly exalted him' (Phil. 2:8, 9).

14:66–72 Peter's denial

Increasingly clearly we have seen Jesus as the Servant, submitting to his Father's will. If Peter represents those who follow Jesus in the way of service, we are here warned how easy it is to stray from that path. The account of Peter's denial has a thoroughly practical purpose. No one was louder than Peter in his protestations of loyalty to Jesus; but words are not enough. What does the servant actually *do* to show his obedience? What came after the big words of verse 29 was in fact failure to keep awake, failure to pray, an instinctive grab for worldly weapons, and a following of Jesus which was neither brave enough to keep right up with him nor wise enough to keep right away from temptation.

So Peter finds himself in the courtyard of the high priest's house, in a situation which is a stark parallel of the one upstairs. Mark no doubt means us to see it that way by planting verse 54 in the previous paragraph and indicating that the two interrogations were happening at once. The tragedy of course is that Peter turns out to be not on the side of Jesus, affirming the truth despite everything, but on the side of the Sanhedrin, denying the truth despite everything.

We can see Satan's subtlety (Luke 22:31) in the way the temptation is set up. Peter's fear for his own safety, his desire to give an acceptable answer, and the angle of the questions, which might have been deliberately calculated to provoke a denial of Jesus, are just what we might expect the great enemy to use. The only defence against him is precisely that, that we *should* expect such methods. Be aware of him, Jesus had said, and keep in touch with your Father – '*Watch* and *pray*, that you may not enter into temptation' (38). Awareness of the actual state of affairs came to Peter when it was too late. He remembered not just what Jesus had said, but 'how' he had said it, that is, all the circumstances of Jesus' agony and the disciples' weakness and presumption. He was prepared to have Mark record his shame so that the realities of temptation might not be ignored by others as they had been by him. Even so, true repentance leads to restoration, as Mark will show (16:7; compare Luke 22:32).

TO THINK OVER: Do we have a realistic awareness of Satan's power and cunning?

15:1–15 Jesus condemned

Great complications beset both the Jews' attempts to have Jesus condemned, and Pilate's to have him released.

Having set up the arrest, the trial, and the false witnesses, the chief priests still have to ensure the actual execution. For that they need Roman authority: hence the dawn meeting to draft the charges with which Jesus will be sent to Pilate (1). Their change of ground at this meeting is ironic. They have condemned him because of his claims to be a *prophet*, which seem to them unsubstantiated and therefore blasphemous (14:64, 65). But the claims to *kingship*, which they lay before Pilate, will lead to a condemnation only if Pilate can be persuaded to think there *is* some substance in them.

Pilate, for his part, first puts the straightforward question of v. 2, arising from the charge – now treason, instead of blasphemy – of which Jesus stands accused (compare Luke 23:2). But for the Roman also a series of complications follows. First, Jesus' reply is not so clear a 'Yes' as to constitute an admission of guilt, or else there would be nothing more to be said. In any case Pilate surely suspects the Jews of bad faith: they are unlikely to care much about protecting the Roman government against traitors! Further, he knows their real motive is envy (10). But, to add yet another factor, he thinks it politic not simply to release Jesus, as he should do, but to release him under the terms of the Passover amnesty (6). This move is the mistake which finally ensures that Pilate loses and the chief priests win (15).

But notice a remarkable thing about the whole complicated business. The early church will in due course be praising God for the fact that the authorities, both Jewish and Roman, spent all this effort simply in the end to bring about 'whatever thy hand and thy plan had predestined' (Acts 4:28). There indeed is matter for praise. We do not forget the solemn truth that the outcome so clearly planned by God, though so complicatedly brought about by his enemies, was the suffering of the Christ. But the outcome of *that*, in its turn, was to be the salvation of sinners: death for Jesus, life for 'Barabbas instead' (11).

THOUGHT: 'I lay down my life ... No one takes it from me, but I lay it down of my own accord. I have power to lay it down...' (John 10:17, 18)

15:16–32 The crucifixion

In Mark's account of the crucifixion, allusions which he himself does not develop can be filled out by comparison with the other Gospels (for example, the reason for v. 24b is given in John 19:23, 24). What he does stress is the royalty and the suffering of the crucified, thrice referred to as king yet each time in mockery.

To the soldiers the title was altogether incongruous. In casting Jesus in the role of a vassal king under Roman sovereignty, complete with purple cloak, crown (probably meant as parody rather than torment), salutations, a 'reed' for sceptre and spitting for the kiss of homage, they 'mocked' (20). The whole parade was ludicrously out of keeping with what seemed to them the facts about him. The chief priests, however, knew better, seeing Jesus as a powerful and dangerous character, though now successfully neutralised. Everything they said about him in verses 31, 32 was true, but in ironic senses they did not intend. They could not see truth the right way round, because they demanded proof before faith. They 'mocked' (31) not in ignorance but in unbelief.

Between these two mocking salutations is a much more complex one – the inscription put on the cross by Pilate (see John 19:19–22). It was factual, in that this was the charge against Jesus. It was also a mockery, contrasting the grandiose title with the helpless victim. It was an insult to the Jews, implying that this poor creature was the kind of king they deserved. Hence their objection in John 19:21. Yet it was in the deepest sense the truth, for he was and is the King of the people of God. Of how many of these layers of meaning was Pilate aware?

In this passage, however, even more important than the kingship is the suffering; and in the suffering of the cross, far more important than its cruelty – it gives us our word 'excruciating', and civilised Romans themselves were appalled by it – is its place in the scheme of redemption. Jesus refused the cup of drugged wine (23) because consciously and deliberately he was going to drink another cup (10:38; 14:36). By not sparing himself, he was to save a multitude of others. In that also his enemies spoke more truly than they knew (31).

TO THINK OVER: How do we respond to the knowledge that our King was a 'helpless' victim?

15:33-39 The death of Jesus

Thrice in irony called a king (18, 26, 32), Jesus in his death receives an even greater title (39).

Mark's deceptively simple style does not draw attention to the truths which lie beneath these largely unwitting testimonies. But we have already noticed that he has an eye for meaningful incidents which his readers are expected to look at through Christian glasses.

So here Jesus' death is preceded by three hours of darkness, which, whether a supernatural event or a natural one miraculously timed, is highly significant. It recalls Exodus 10:21, 22 and Amos 8:9, 10, and is set side by side with the next event, the 'cry of dereliction' which quotes Ps. 22:1. The Son's (and the world's) separation from the light of the Father's face is expressed first visibly, then audibly. The unity of the Trinity cannot be broken; yet in whatever sense Isaiah 59:2 is fulfilled in 2 Corinthians 5:21, and Deuteronomy 21:23 in Galatians 3:13, in that sense the Son is at this moment cut off from the Father.

Just before the moment of death Jesus utters another cry, very probably the triumphant 'It is finished' of John 19:30. Again Mark sets, without explanation, sign beside word: Jesus' death-cry and the tearing of the Temple curtain. Whether this was the curtain before the Holy Place, or (more likely) the 'second curtain' (Heb. 9:3) which screened the Holy of Holies, its rending points to the destruction of the Temple itself, of the whole Old Testament system, and of the barriers which exclude sinners from God's presence and Gentiles from his people (Heb. 9:1–10:22).

And the reactions of those who stood by the cross? Some, though sympathising with the suffering man (the 'vinegar' was cheap wine, offered in kindness), could not see what was really happening – another aspect of the darkness. But the centurion, whatever pagan meaning he may have had in mind, saw what he could only describe as the death of 'the Son of God'. And Mark surely intends his readers to see that with these words his Gospel comes full circle (compare 1:1, 11), and to read them in the fullest Christian sense. As verses 33, 34 dramatise the suffering of the Christ, and verses 37, 38 the salvation which is thereby obtained for us, verse 39 with its implications is the response of worship and service we therefore owe to him.

THOUGHT: 'It is in the cry of dereliction that the full horror of man's sin stands revealed' (C.E.B. Cranfield)

15:40–47 The burial of Jesus

Both for Jesus' chief enemies and for his chief followers, it is enough and more than enough to have seen him dying. It is left to lesser characters in the drama to see him dead. A group of women remain, including some who quite possibly are not only friends and followers of Jesus, but also related to him and to several of the twelve. But in this last extremity those one would have thought closest to him are, sadly, far from him (14:50; though his mother and John stayed almost to the end, John 19:26, 27).

The chief priests seem also to have departed, having achieved their object. As the strange darkness clears to give three more hours of daylight before sunset and the coming of the Sabbath, officialdom is seen to be represented now by three people. The emergence of Joseph of Arimathaea as a disciple of Jesus testifies to a real if belated courage, now doing for Jesus what Jews consider ought to be done (the body taken from cross to tomb before the onset of night and the Sabbath) but what those closer to him will not or cannot do. Roman custom, on the other hand, completed the criminal's degradation by leaving him unburied, indeed rotting on the cross. Pilate's exercise of his prerogative of granting the body to the relatives for burial, unusual in a case of treason, testifies to his suspicions about the whole affair, and perhaps to his sense of guilt over the condemning of an innocent man. The centurion, having declared that Jesus is truly Son of God, now testifies that he is equally truly dead.

In fact from one point of view the whole passage is about *testimony*. The pooled testimony of all these people concerning Jesus is that he really *has* died, and he is buried in *this* tomb (47). The witnesses either have nothing to gain, or are testifying to something they wish were not true, or speak as military men with authority; and so we take their witness to be truthful. For only a *real* death and burial assure his people that their own former life has *really* come to an end and been replaced by a new life in him (Rom. 6:4).

THOUGHT: 'Unless a grain of wheat falls into the earth and dies, it remains alone; but if it dies, it bears much fruit' (John 12:24).

16:1–8 The end of the Gospel?

Mark completes his Gospel with the resurrection, for him a fact as real as every other great event he has recounted. This paragraph is bound closely to those that precede. It is the women who saw Jesus dead (15:40) and buried (15:47) who now hear his resurrection announced, the tomb earlier occupied and sealed is the one now open and empty; he 'who was crucified ... has risen' (6). If what went before is historically true, then so (we are meant to understand) is this, although it be the greatest and most incredible miracle of all time.

This final great fact has, to Mark's mind, one overwhelming result (8); and it leads us to consider the matter of how he ends the Gospel. After verse 8 there is added, in some manuscripts, a short ending of one or two sentences; in others, a longer ending, often now printed as verses 9–20; presumably because it was thought more suitable that the closing words of the Gospel should express joy, faith, or challenge. But if (as some think) Mark actually meant to end at 16:8, what was in his mind in so doing?

A concordance-study of words denoting amazement, awe, and fear will show that these are what he constantly uses in describing reactions to the way God reveals himself in the gospel story. Men are astonished and afraid at the deeds, words, and very appearance of Jesus. Beyond that, they will tremble at the revelation that the Son of God is prepared to be also the suffering Servant (10:32–34), and still more at the teaching that his followers also will have to tread the way of the cross (8:34).

From Mark's point of view, then, it is altogether fitting that when *his* Gospel ends by declaring that *the* gospel in fact goes on, with Jesus still inexorably 'going before' (7), the human reaction is trembling, astonishment, and fear (8). Nothing could be further from the triumphalist faith of some of today's churches. Yet paradoxically, Mark's ending – as abrupt as his beginning – strikes the note of encouragement for suffering Christians: their trials are foreknown, allowed for, and in the plan and control of the God who did after all, after Calvary, raise his Son from the dead.

TO THINK OVER: Has our familiarity with the gospel message robbed us of the ability to react in the way those who met Jesus did?

16:9–20 An anonymous postscript

These additional verses are not in Mark's style, and the join at verse 9 is untidy. But the unknown writer's object is clear enough. Either he knew this Gospel did not originally end at 16:8 (that is, Mark wrote an ending which was later lost), or he knew it did, but felt it should not; so he supplied vs. 9–20 to round it off. He might well have believed that a proper Gospel, like the evangelistic sermons in Acts, ought to include human (and not just angelic) testimony to the risen Christ.

That at any rate is the content of this postscript. It describes resurrection appearances found in different form, and at much greater length, in the other Gospels (see John 20:11–18; Luke 24:13–35; Matt. 28:16–20, etc.). The miraculous signs which it says will be seen in the New Testament church are all (except the poison-drinking) to be found in Acts. It ends with the twin statements of verses 19, 20: Jesus goes up, to sit on the throne of heaven, while his church goes out, to preach to the people of earth. Jesus' 'sitting' means 'not the posture of his body, but the majesty of his empire' (Calvin, quoted by Cranfield), and we know therefore that so far from his ascension separating him from his people, it enables him now to wield his power universally, as by his Spirit he works 'with them' (20).

All this, though doubtless not part of the original Gospel of Mark, is nonetheless a compendium of gospel truth, and sums up a good deal of the earliest Christian belief. In fact, its chief value may be to focus our attention on the matter of belief and unbelief. First it stresses the latter, in a way found elsewhere only in the Thomas story (John 20:24–29). This leads up to the crux of the passage: for faith, which the apostles themselves have found so hard, is at the heart of the message they must now preach (16). Will their hearers believe in Christ, or not? If they do, then the faith which leads to salvation (16) will be followed by action on their own part ('and be baptised'), and confirmation on God's part ('signs', 17, 18, 20).

CHALLENGE: 'They went forth and preached everywhere' – what are we doing to carry on the work they began?

Questions for further study and discussion on Mark 14:53–16:20

1. Trace the themes of service and suffering through Mark's Gospel. What do you learn about their place in the Christian life? How far does today's church exemplify Jesus' teaching?

2. What do we learn from Peter about facing temptation?

3. Our modern world (and much of the church) has given up belief in a personal devil. What are the consequences of this? How far is it true that the devil's greatest achievement has been to convince men that he does not exist? How should we explain the biblical teaching to someone with no Christian background?

4. Consider the relationship between God's plans and man's actions in the events leading to the crucifixion. What do we learn from this?

5. The suggestion that Jesus was not really dead is still heard. What would Mark have made of this? How does his account help us to counter the charge? (See, too, Acts 2:29; 1 Cor. 15:4.)

6. Do you think that our modern worship gives adequate expression to 'awe, amazement and fear'? What would you change in your own patterns and structure of worship?

7. Should we expect to see 'signs' accompanying those who believe? If so, what might they be?

8. Jesus chose twelve 'to be with him'. Having read Mark, compare Jesus' methods with ours. What do you consider are the most important components in a programme of training for the Christian ministry?